BLINDED BY HIS SHADOW

by TAMMY ZIMMERMAN

BLINDED BY HIS SHADOW

DISCOVERING THE POWERFUL LEGACY BEHIND THE ORDINARY LIFE OF JOSEPH T. ZIMMERMAN

BLINDED BY HIS SHADOW
Copyright © 2012 by Tammy Zimmerman

Library of Congress Control Number: 2012914429

ISBN-13: 978-0-9858733-0-1 (Pbk.)

Interior Book Design by Tiffany Hiebert
Cover Design by Hannah Gleghorn

Cover photograph:
Soldiers of 255th Regiment, 63rd Infantry Division in Waldenburg, Germany, April 1945, *courtesy of National Archives*

Author photograph by Audra Buchanan

Manufactured in the United States of America
2012—First Adico Publishing Paperback Edition

Adico Publishing
1100 East 103rd Street South
Mulvane, Kansas 67110

Visit us online at www.BlindedByHisShadow.com

To Dad,
who will always be my hero

CONTENTS

AUTHOR'S NOTE

As a ten-year-old, I lay across my parents' bed staring at an old, slightly fuzzy black and white photo of my young grandma standing next to a man in overalls. His jovial smile proved a love for life. The picture of a man unknown to me and unmentioned by others silently stood on my dad's dresser. Who was he? What was he like? I studied the photograph, trying to read—something about the past.

No one said much about my Grandpa Zimmerman that I remember. He was like a ghost. Someone who *seemed* to have made a deep impact on all who knew him but whose memory was just out of reach, floating into one's mind but with no substance. By my mid-twenties, I could remember hearing only three facts about him: he had played the accordion; he had supposedly been hit on the head with a rifle butt during World War II as German prisoners of war broke free; and he had died of a brain tumor at the age of thirty-eight, leaving his wife and seven children behind. These were quickly mentioned and then passed over as if revealing any more information would force the teller to reach too deeply into a painful past.

I cannot think of a time when both literature and history were not my passions. In school I read far ahead in those particular textbooks, anxious to discover what happened next (to the detriment of math and science, I must say). Five years ago, I picked up *Citizen Soldiers* by Stephen Ambrose. Though I rarely re-read a book, it was my second time through the account of the Allied Army's post-Normandy invasion of France and Germany. Military strategy, details of hedgerow fighting and maps of the Siegfried Line kept me awake far into the night and caused some family members to question my sanity. While in the midst of Screaming Mimis and trench foot, I suddenly recalled the family story of Grandpa Zimmerman and the German POW breakout. German. POWs. That meant…

I rushed to find his wallet that Grandma had given to Dad just a couple of months previously. Within the folds rested a small copy of his discharge paper. Squinting at the tiny print, I barely made out the words Central Europe, Rhineland, Combat Infantry Badge. He had been there! Why I had not put the facts together before is beyond me.

That began a journey not unlike a scavenger hunt to discover pieces of a thousand piece puzzle. (And I am quite sure that even at this point, more than a few pieces are still hiding.) Thousands of internet searches yielded one small victory after another. Once, after weeks of no progress, a picture of a Nazi flag, found in a German city's rubble by a passing infantryman, along with a list of the man's buddies who had signed it popped up on the screen. Joe Zimmerman's name appeared on the list.

The 63rd Infantry Division Association provided invaluable information, pictures and names of men who had served in Grandpa's unit. I regularly poured over the Association's order form, making check marks for maps, morning reports and historical accounts before sending off a check and excitedly waiting for a package to arrive in the mail.

Many phone calls to veterans began with the words, "You

don't know me, but my Grandpa served with you." Some men remembered; some could not. When I asked about the signed Nazi flag, one sweet man replied, "Well, this is your lucky day. I own that flag!"

Letters were constantly at the forefront of my quest. I knew Grandpa had written home while overseas, and I wanted to hear his "voice." I could find out all *about* him, but I wanted to *know him*. During one conversation, an aunt mentioned that the family had sometimes submitted his letters to the local newspaper, like so many families did at that time. Hours of scanning microfilmed newspapers in an uncomfortable, straight-back library chair uncovered more pieces of the mystery—notices, interviews, a poem and five letters. I spared my quiet, fellow-researchers from witnessing a song and dance for joy. My family was not so fortunate.

Grandma and I dug through drawers, closets and boxes in my dogmatic opinion that she must have kept *something* he wrote to her. After several years, I finally gave up the search as a lost cause. Then she said in a recent visit, "I was going through my nightstand and found an envelope." You would have thought she had found gold the way my heart started beating. In a way, she had.

My initial intention for this research was never to write a book. I simply enjoyed learning and searching, and I thought a book would be impossible. But God had other plans for this project. Thankfully, He placed in my path people, ideas, websites and books to guide me through the journey. As the One Who is my eternal Hope and my constant Friend, the Lord Jesus Christ is the first One I must thank.

Thus begins the long list of appreciation to those who have given invaluable support. My mom, Barb Zimmerman, is the best editor an author could ever desire. From my repetitive first grade descriptions of "It was fun" to high school and college research papers, she has read and edited every painful and a few rare not-so-painful pages that I have produced. Many times her encouragement kept me from boxing up all of the research and storing it in a deep, dark closet.

When I think of Darrell Zimmerman, my daddy, I cannot find words to adequately express the gratefulness I owe to him. Though he lost his father at the young age of fourteen, he became to me the very picture of an ideal dad. Never in the forefront, he served and loved his family unconditionally and gave steady support as I pursued my dreams, no matter how crazy they sometimes were. Nothing could surpass the respect I have for him.

For enduring the questions and hours of digging through her house, my Grandma Martina Zimmerman truly deserves a medal. She was always patient with my research, though I am sure that more than once she was relieved when I returned home. More importantly, however, is the fact that she stood strong when her life crumbled in order to raise her and Joe's seven children and run the farm. I admire the strength of this German lady.

The thought of writing a book may seem glamorous, but actually doing it is not. Caleb King, the most wonderful man God could have given to me, willingly made countless wake up phone calls at 4:00 a.m. and convinced me that I had indeed wanted to leave the comfort of my warm bed in order to drink excessive amounts of coffee and type on the computer. He always encouraged and supported me when I began to question the sanity of beginning such a project.

Many times, I found it necessary to bounce ideas off people who would give an objective opinion along with moral support for the endeavor. Two individuals who never failed to give this were my sisters, Christy Gimben and Tracey Hager. Also, Gail Moseley deserves a gold star for all the times she put her red pen to my writing.

The research for this project would have been impossible were it not for the 63rd Infantry Division Association, for its historian William (Bill) Scott and for its webmaster Fred Clinton. I have benefited from the hours of work they volunteered to compile documents and information. From this resource, I learned the names of several men who had served in Grandpa's Company L of the 255th Regiment. A special thank you also goes to these veterans (and their wives) first for their service to this country and also for granting me the privilege of hearing their stories.

Other people who graciously shared their time and memories are those who knew Joe Zimmerman the best—his sisters, brothers and children. Each person had a unique and special relationship with this man, and they gave me the gift of my own indirect relationship with my grandfather. It is a priceless treasure that I will forever cherish.

Grandpa Zimmerman's young death was tragic, but it was his life that fascinated me. I want to tell this story so that his memory will never die. I want to tell the story of a man I never knew.

TAMMY ZIMMERMAN
Mulvane, Kansas
August 2, 2012

DEAR GRANDPA

Dear Grandpa who I'll never see
I wish I could have known you—
Who'd let me climb upon your knee
Who'd catch the kiss I'd thrown you.

When I think of the stolen days
We weren't allowed to share,
I look up to the heaven's rays
And hope to see you there.

God hears our prayers before we pray.
Perhaps He's heard mine too
Of how I long to live the day
When I at last see you.

Until the day I find you there
In God's Home above you,
These last few words I want to share:
Grandfather, I love you.

TRACEY [ZIMMERMAN] HAGER
September 3, 1992

Joseph P. Zimmerman

PART ONE

CHAPTER ONE

"[G]reat lives don't always seem great while we're living them. They may seem embarrassingly regular."

Beth Moore[1]

The night hung cold and damp as *L Company's 2nd Platoon**
moved out.[2] Fewer than forty men stumbled through the dark
winter night, several of them having joined the unit just that
day.[3] Carefully picking their way up the southern side of the hill
through woods thick with underbrush and mud, they navigated
through terrain that was difficult in the daytime and all but impassible at night. Intermittent enemy gunfire pierced the stillness. The men were not able to see the enemy, but they nervously
heard and felt their movements all the same. Finally, the platoon
reached the destination. They relieved Company I and took their
turn holding this hill, which had been won seven days earlier.[4]

---

* All referenced military units under which Joseph Zimmerman served will be
italicized for clarification.

Finding newly abandoned foxholes, the men, some still strangers to each other, settled in for what little rest they could manage in the remaining night of February 13, 1945. Among these defenders was Private Joseph T. Zimmerman.[5]

Crossing the railroad tracks on February 6, *Love Company* had attacked the eastern hill in the Bliesbrucken Wald (woods). Thus began the *255th Regiment's* attempt to drive the Germans out of Bliesbruck, north of the forest, and to silence the random shelling coming from the town. Through enemy machine gun and mortar fire, attacks, counterattacks and the general din and confusion of battle, the men persisted and gained control of the day's objective. Other than an occasional outbreak of fighting, the next few days were filled with the tedious task of holding the hill; the next few nights were punctuated with the uncertain task of conducting patrols across the swollen Blies River.[6]

As February 15 arrived, Joe Zimmerman began his second day on the front lines. At 6:15 a.m., the explosion of a single artillery round suddenly interrupted the silence of the foggy, pre-dawn morning.[7] For the next several hours, the distant staccato of machine guns, the thunder of mortar and artillery fire and the short blasts of schu-mine explosions filled the air.[8] Still with the *2nd Platoon*, Zimmerman continued to hold the defensive positions on the hill up which they had struggled two nights previously. He was not a part of this day's battle, but across the valley, he could see and hear the conflict for the two eastern hills.[9]

The *255th Regiment* had ordered that its *3rd Battalion* seize the three hills in the Bliesbrucken Wald; two hills remained on that morning. Company K met little resistance for the far eastern hill, but I Company experienced great difficulty on the hill closest to the defensive *2nd Platoon*.[10] Soldiers picked their way through extensive schu-mine fields (land mines named for the fact that, when stepped on, they bounced just high enough to rip off a man's lower leg and shoe.) Past the mines, they had to confront an enemy who was well protected under bunkers six to eight feet wide that were covered and camouflaged by heavy logs. The thick underbrush took away the advancing soldier's opportunity to lie on the ground and fight from a prone position; he had to stand exposed to the intense enemy fire. At 9:00 a.m., the Germans counterattacked and pinned down one platoon of Company I. The platoon had allowed the enemy to close in not only because they had difficulty seeing the advance but also because they were confused by the U.S. Army coats that some Germans soldiers wore.[11]

Throughout the day, Company K, with the help of the 1st Platoon of *Love Company*, reached their goal. However, Company I, supported by *Love's* 3rd Platoon, suffered heavy casualties* and needed covering fire to withdraw from the ground for which they had fought so bitterly.[12]

Soldiers on the front line did not know the details about the day's battle although "scuttlebutt" had a way of getting around in the ranks. Zimmerman's company had been fortunate in the fact that the two platoons involved in the action had only seven casualties during the day (three lightly wounded, two killed in action and two sick.)[13] He settled in for another night in the foxhole, soaked by rain and sustained by K-rations.[14] The bright flares of rockets and the boom of mortars continued in the east and west until midnight as the infantry kept attempting to take the Bliesbrucken Wald.[15]

---

* The term "casualty of war" is often equated with killed in action. Throughout this book, the author uses the technical definition of "casualty," which refers to all reasons a soldier might involuntarily leave military service, whether temporarily or permanently. This includes illness, killed, missing or wounded in action.

The next morning, February 16, Joe "feasted" on the ever-present K-rations for breakfast.[16] He might have been lucky enough to pick a rations pack intended for breakfast, but one never knew until it was open. Today, he did not have the luxury of watching the battle from a distance. Although he had already experienced sporadic fighting, this would be his first full-fledged battle.

Regimental Headquarters ordered three of its companies to take the hill to the east on which Company I had suffered and been defeated the previous day. *Company L* and two other companies moved into position during the morning. As 11:00 a.m. came, Company B started the attack across the woods. *L Company* waited. An hour passed before they moved out, but once they started, nothing stopped them.[17]

Authors Jeffrey J. Clarke and Robert Ross Smith relate in their extensive book, *Riviera To the Rhine*, how one soldier felt as he went into battle.

> Recalling his reactions going into combat for the first time, one former infantryman described his emotions as "taciturn; diffident; frightened, almost meek; mechanically going forward." …conversation languished and tension steadily mounted. Rifles, ammunition belts, and hand grenades were mechanically checked and rechecked; helmets clamped down a bit snugger; chin straps tightened. The sudden sound of small-arms fire and artillery electrified each man, paralyzing him for a few seconds as he automatically hunched closer to the ground. Then, as the unit moved forward to "the objective," the noise of exploding shells grew deafening, each one causing the earth to shake and pieces of dirt, metal, and wood to whine overhead. The tangy smell of burnt powder filled

the air and the sounds of men screaming and officers cursing and yelling were quickly lost in the general din. Then suddenly the attack was over – the goal reached, the objective secured. At that point, he recalled, "the fear we had felt descended on us like an avalanche, leaving us only cold and wet and exhausted."[18]

In little over an hour, *Love Company* destroyed two of the fortified bunkers and crossed the bridge to the left of Company I.[19] The two forces joined and met with Company B opposite them. The three units successfully won the hill in just a couple of hours, the same hill from which Company I had withdrawn in defeat the day before.[20] The men dug their foxholes in the muddy earth to defend the area.[21] Rain came again that night, but its gloomy effects were diminished by the enjoyment of their victory and a "hot" supper brought up from the rear. Though the food was cool by the time it reached them, it was still better than K-rations.[22]

The next couple of days, the men stayed in the same location, seeing little offensive action but receiving random mortar fire from the Germans in the town of Bliesbrucken. Explosions in the trees sent lethal shards of wood and metal raining down from above and shook the ground beneath, causing young, strong soldiers to huddle in their foxholes. One moment the forest hung in deadly silence, all sounds and sights muffled by a dense fog; the next moment a noise such as never heard before and a fear such as never felt briefly reigned, then stillness came once again.[23] Intermittent shouts of "Medic!" interrupted the eerie quietness.

Finally, B Company crossed the rushing Blies River to silence the German mortar team.[24] The Americans typically had no problem eliminating such a position; they simply called in artillery fire. However, this time the Germans had strategically set up in the middle of a cemetery, and even when surrounded by death, the Allies held a certain respect for the buried dead.[25]

Private Zimmerman was now a combat veteran; he had survived his first days. The next few weeks his unit held the front lines, wherever the colonels and generals decided that should be. It meant long days with little action, days in which he spent most of his time cramped with another fellow in a small hole in the ground, days in which he passed the time talking or thinking.

June 6, 1944—Across the world announcers interrupted radio broadcasts with a news flash from the Supreme Allied Headquarters. "Under the command of General Eisenhower, Allied naval forces, supported by strong air forces, began landing Allied armies this morning on the northern coast of France."[26]

The war had been raging for two and a half years, and the Allies had just accomplished the unfathomable—they had landed on a strip of beach in Normandy, France, in an invasion of the European continent. Logistically, it did not make sense. Armies needed ports not only for their troop ships but also for supply ships required for such a vast force. General Eisenhower thought differently, however, and with American boldness he chose a sandy beach for the greatest offensive in history. The casualties numbered high; the bloodshed was incomprehensible; but the Allies had landed. The French countryside was a natural defense against attack, and the Germans, having occupied the country for two years, certainly strengthened those barriers and used them to their advantage. Thick, tangled hedgerows surrounding each French field hindered men and tanks from advancing quickly, and many times stopped them completely.[27] What openings there were through these hedgerows, the enemy covered with artillery fire, mortar fire, machine gun fire and mine fields.

In the days and weeks following the landing, the Allies progressed slowly through Normandy. American ingenuity was tested to the limit in the attempts to find a way around, through or over the obstacles. However, on July 27, their intense fighting and bombing were rewarded as the Allies finally broke through German lines.[28]

A new kind of warfare was developed in that summer of 1944. Out of necessity and through trial and error, the Allies began to use the Army Air Force not only to drop bombs on the enemy, but also to act as forward observers for the infantry. Extreme accuracy was gained through close radio communication between the pilots and the ground forces because of their combined effort.[29] After claiming victory through the tedious hedgerow fighting in Normandy, the Allies essentially won the battle for France. They advanced through the country with staggering swiftness as the Germans fell back as quickly as possible, occasionally turning to fight the invading Allies at one of Hitler's insane orders. Major Charles Cawthorn, an officer in General Patton's Third Army believed that the German retreat was not like "a game of Allied hounds coursing the German hare, [but like hunting] a wounded tiger into the bush; the tiger turning now and again to slash at its tormentors, each slash drawing blood."[30]

———————

While the world was at war, life on the home front was normal and abnormal at the same time. Week after week more sons, brothers, husbands and boyfriends left their homes and families at Uncle Sam's terse orders. Local newspapers were filled with notifications of who had been drafted, who was leaving for basic training, who was promoted, who had changed addresses and who had been injured or killed. Soldiers, sailors and Marines wrote letters home, and many times these letters, too, would be included in the paper so the community could keep up with their boys away from home. However, in rural western Kansas, like countless areas across the country, the days continued much as they always had. For the Zimmerman family, life was hard but rewarding. It was a life classically American.

Both Theodore and Rosalie [Heier] Zimmerman immigrated to the United States of America as children. They had lived most of their lives in their adopted country, and Ted had even served in the army during World War I. America was their country, and they fully embraced the opportunity given them to own a farm and raise a family.

As devoted Catholics, family was important to the Zimmermans. While living in a sod house, Ted and Rosalie welcomed their first daughter. Soon their family grew, and they moved to another home. On October 30, 1923, the doctor was called to help with the birth of a third child—this time a son—Joseph Theodore Zimmerman.

Throughout the years as their family became larger, they experienced joy and sorrow, blessings and hardships. Later in life Rosalie nearly died in a difficult childbirth. Although both she and baby Emma lived, Emma suffered from cerebral palsy, and, in the two years of her life, she could never hold her head up or sit by herself. When Rosalie was eight months pregnant with her next child, Emma stopped breathing. Her mother helplessly held the child's lifeless body as Ted rushed in from the field.[31]

But, amidst the trials, the couple also knew the relief of raising an otherwise healthy family. In 1942, when Rosalie was 43 and Ted was 50, their fourteenth child, Rowena (known as Rene) was born. Because of the difference in ages, Ted and Rosalie's children were almost like two separate families—an older and a younger group—but they all grew close to each other.[32]

Ted and Rosalie's thirteen children, all first-generation Americans, shared in the hard work of their German parents. On their four-hundred-acre farm, fields had to be tended, cows milked, fences mended, the large family fed. Life was certainly not easy, but it was definitely good.

For the most part, they liked their neighbors, and their neighbors respected them. Only a few families in the area allowed their prewar, anti-German sentiment to cloud their thinking. Despite these occasional prejudices against the "Germans," the Zimmermans knew the truth. They were Americans through and through.

They received an opportunity to prove this patriotism in July of '44 as they offered their first-born son back to the country that had given them so much. Joe was not surprised at the orders from Uncle Sam; he was young, healthy and desperately needed by a country nearly three years into a world war. At a time when people tended to disdain a man if he was not serving the country in uniform, Joe might have even been grateful or excited that he had received his draft notice. But the people closest to him did not share his excitement. His parents knew war and feared what they knew; his sisters did *not* know war and feared what they did not know; his girlfriend, under her quiet strength, simply feared losing him.

Saturday nights were nights of fun and relaxation when the Zimmerman kids headed to town for a movie or a dance. Most of the time, the older kids went together, picking up friends along the way. One of Joe's good friends Lawrence Dreher started dating Joe's sister Johanna, and all three of them would go out together.[33] Sometimes the car was so crowded with the Zimmerman kids and their dates that the girls could only crowd in by sitting on their boyfriends' laps.[34]

At one of these Saturday night dances, Joe met Martina Ziegler. They began dating and soon became serious about their future together. Joe tenderly devoted himself to his girl. Now he was leaving with the possibility of never returning. Not only would this war affect the future of a young couple very much in love, but it also came at a tragic time for Martina.

On July 27, 1944, the *Gove County Advocate* published its weekly list of young men bound for military induction the following week. Joseph T. Zimmerman's name appeared on the list. That same paper held another notification.

MRS. ADAM ZIEGLER RITES HELD AT COLLYER TUESDAY

Funeral services were conducted Tuesday morning from St. Michael's Church for Mrs. Adam Ziegler, who passed away at her home south east of Quinter at noon Sunday following a week's serious illness. She is survived by her husband and the following children, who were all able to be with her during her last illness: Adam and Martina of the home; John, Alex and Excavior [*sic*] of Collyer; Joe of Colorado; Henry of Grainfield and Mrs. Adam Selensky of Park.[35]

Martina's mother suffered a stroke at the age of sixty-seven, and at twenty-one years old, Martina became responsible for running her father's household. They held the funeral on July 25, two days after her mother's death. Three weeks later on August 9, Joe left for basic training.

With German stoicism, Joe's girlfriend, parents and all his siblings—Katherine (Kay) who lived in Arkansas with her husband, Theresa, Johanna, Mary, Fabian, Edmund (Eddie), Celestina (Sally), twins Alberta (Bert) and Albina (Bina), Fidelis (Dale), Loretta, and one-year-old Rowena (Rene)—said goodbye. Joe left for induction into the United States Army for "Enlistment for the duration of the War or other emergency plus six months, subject to the discretion of the President or otherwise according to law."[36] Later, Alberta voiced her emotions during the next few years, "To me it was a really sad time; that's why I never watch a war movie. It just brings back those times that were so hard for Mom and Dad. Even if you're young, things make an impression on you."[37]

Tyler, Texas, was hot, dusty, full of mosquitoes, and perfect for a U.S. Army Infantry Replacement Training Center named Camp Fannin. From May of 1943 to December of 1945, Camp Fannin trained 200,000 men to be funneled into the war effort; and for the next seventeen weeks, it would be Joe's new home. This farmer-turned-soldier learned to work with new tools such as a M1 .30 Caliber Carbine, Browning Automatic Rifle (BAR), .50 Caliber Browning Machine Gun (M2), hand grenades, and mortars.[38] For a country boy, guns were nothing new, but guns being fired at him were altogether different. According to Colonel James E. Hatcher, the men trained with live ammunition so that "each infantryman [would] become accustomed to the presence of artillery and small arms fire in his immediate vicinity."[39] Casualties in basic training were known to occur, but Joe obviously learned to keep his head down.

As Zimmerman prepared for war, the Allies continued to advance through France. They reached Paris on August 23, but victory did not come without a cost. Already Allied casualties in France numbered almost 210,000, and nearly 40,000 of that total number were killed in action. Two-thirds of the casualties were American boys.[40] The Germans rushed to the French/

German border to prepare a defense of their homeland, and the Americans followed with incredible speed. That speed soon changed.[41]

CHAPTER TWO

"[D]ead men everywhere look pathetic and lonely. You feel as if you would like them to be alive and the war over."

Lieutenant Charles Stockell when arriving at Normandy June 7, 1944[1]

"Give me your tired, your poor,
Your huddled masses yearning to breathe free,
The wretched refuse of your teeming shore.
Send these, the homeless, tempest-tost to me,
I lift my lamp beside the golden door!"

Emma Lazarus, "The New Colossus" engraved on the Statue of Liberty

The successful Allied advance of July and August had been dizzying. The army had moved forward six hundred kilometers in August alone. However, progress then slowed drastically, and throughout the rest of the year, they gained a mere thirty-five kilometers.[2] Armies need supplies, and the supply lines had difficulty keeping up with the swiftness of the army. In October, the Allies finally caught up with the German Army as they stopped to set up a defense of their homeland's border. In November, rains came, bogging down vehicles and troops even more, and the infamously cold winter of 1944-45 began. In December, the Battle of the Bulge raged.

———————

A portion of the Ardennes Forest spread across the Belgium border into northern France. The area was not considered important; it was not where the action was located; it was the area commanding generals gave to the weaker Allied units to defend. The quietness of the Ardennes convinced the officers and soldiers that the Germans in the area would cause them no harm. To Adolf Hitler, a man crazed with victory at all costs, it was the ideal place to launch an attack.[3]

By December 16, 1944, the soldiers on the front lines suffered from the bitter cold, wind and snow. That day, however, the elements of winter were the least of their problems. The Germans began an artillery barrage and a battle that would leave a deep scar on every survivor. German SS troops forcefully attacked in a desperate attempt to infiltrate the Allied lines and cut off the men in the Ardennes. Even by the end of the very first day, events did not go according to German plans. The wooded hills made a quick conquest difficult—and then there was the dedicated spirit of the American soldiers. These men who were not supposed to be the "fightin'est" units of Uncle Sam's Army would just not give up.[4]

The determination of those infantrymen allowed the Allied army to survive the Battle of the Bulge, but it was at the troops' expense. Approximately 610,000 men fought in the Ardennes

Forest from December 16 to January 15. From that number, the Allies lost nearly 81,000 in casualties; the Germans lost anywhere from 80,000 to 104,000.[5] A total of 160,000-184,000 men died or were wounded, missing or captured; 160,000-184,000 husbands, brothers, sons, nephews, friends, uncles gave their life as a gift that Christmas of 1944; 160,000-184,000 families, mothers and fathers, daughters and sons, wives and girlfriends, sisters and brothers received a knock on the door, a telegram, a sincere apology; 160,000-184,000 guns were suddenly silenced. Now, the Allies urgently needed replacements.

———

Pvt. Joseph Zimmerman was a pleasant visitor in our office Friday. He has taken his boot training at Camp Fannin, Texas and after his furlough with home folks here will go to Nescho, Mo., for further duties. Joe tells us that the gang from this neck of the woods got together once in a while down at Camp Fannin and really enjoyed themselves visiting. Quite a few of the fellows came home recently on furlough and are also being transferred elsewhere. — *The Gove County Advocate*[6]

Joe had survived his six weeks of basic training and eleven weeks of advanced infantry training at Camp Fannin. For a farm boy, it really was not much more difficult than normal life, and, actually, it was a whole lot more fun. In the army he did not have to squeeze in time to go shooting; shooting had become his main purpose in life, his only purpose. Everyone knew war was deadly serious, but in basic, it was a game.

The infantry ordered Joe to report at Fort Meade, Maryland, but gave him a ten-day "delay enroute" just in time for

Christmas.[7] A whole ten days he spent with family and friends whom he had not seen in over four months, yet a meager ten days before he left for war, possibly never to return. He filled the time probably teasing his sisters, gathering with friends, and, of course, seeing Martina. Before he left, Ted and Rosalie gathered their family at the photographer's in the nearby town of Oakley to take what might have been their last family picture. All too soon, Joe boarded the eastbound train. The Battle of the Bulge was raging, and the generals demanded more men.

Zimmerman, Joseph T., Private First Class—rifle, new clothes, ammo belt, bayonet, sleeping bag, gas mask, canteen, mess kit, barracks bag, first aid kit, entrenching tool, raincoat. Pick up your gear. Stand in the next line. Move along, men; move along. At Fort Meade the soldiers received gear, provisions and last instructions before crossing the Atlantic. Time spent there was short; there was no time to lose. Some men did receive a two-day pass to visit nearby Washington, D.C., and this small-town kid might have had the opportunity to see the sights in the nation's capital before leaving his country.[8]

From Fort Meade, Maryland, to Fort Kilmer, New Jersey, Joe traveled. Typically, troops spent a week at Fort Kilmer waiting for embarkation, and, again, some of them received a two-day pass for nearby New York City.[9] In this man's army, soldiers learned to hurry up and wait; but, finally, one black winter night, Joe boarded the *Queen Mary*, thus beginning his journey to Europe.[10] Did he crowd in with the thousands of men on the ship's deck in silent reflection, moving toward the unknown, eyes straining through the inky wartime darkness to catch a last glimpse of home?

Barely forty years earlier, Ted and Rosalie had come to this country; they had entered the harbor under the shadow of the Statue of Liberty, America's greatest symbol of freedom. Now their son was going back to the old country to *be* the statue of liberty, America's greatest gift for freedom.

CHAPTER THREE

"Many thousands of men have stood by the rail watching the shores of America slowly recede over the horizon into yesterdays. Each of those many thousands has had his own pensive moments as his eyes clung to that shore line. Perhaps it was to be the last visual link with the lives and persons with whom his years had been associated. He strove by means of some unrecognized force to hold it to him, and through its visual presence, to bring again to him the sense of nearness of well remembered faces somewhere on that distant shore. Turning the eyes away after the parting gaze at America seemed to break a magic chain."

Colonel James Hatcher[1]

The *Queen Mary* carried her precious cargo across the Atlantic, carefully watching for German U-boats. The Liberty Ship had her own interesting history. Like many other wartime vessels, she had been a passenger ship converted into a troop ship. She could hold 15,000 soldiers on each trip, and delivered one such load to the beaches of Normandy on D-Day just six months prior to January, 1945. Her job was to transport troops to the ports of the United Kingdom and to return wounded soldiers, German prisoners, and occasionally GI brides and children to North America. Three times, Winston Churchill was a passenger on the *Queen Mary*.[2]

Troops mingled about the ship for the seven-day voyage. Constantly wearing their Mae West life jackets and steel helmets in case of an attack, each man resembled a cross between an over-stuffed teddy bear and a battle-ready soldier. They spent the time in daily calisthenics, resting, talking, joining a card or dice game, reading, writing letters home and standing in the ever-present chow line.[3] The chow line, of course, was optional depending on if a man felt like eating. Up and down, back and forth, up and down, moving, rolling, tossing, up and down. Maybe Joe never got his "sea legs," maybe he felt hopelessly vulnerable in the midst of the ocean's vast emptiness, or maybe he hated the nights of being crammed into the hold with fifteen thousand other men stacked in bunks five high.[4] Whatever the reason, Joe's local newspaper later reported he had "no desire whatsoever to again travel by water—in fact Joe says it will suit him just fine if he never has to look at an ocean again."[5] Finally, the port of Gourock, Scotland, welcomed the men to land.[6]

Joe probably preferred the familiar clack and clatter of the train that took them across Scotland and through England. But once more in the night's gift of darkness, the men boarded a ship, this one much older and smaller, to cross the English Channel. The trip was brief. The destination offered no port; this destination had only battle-scarred beaches; this destination had been secured and made safe at the cost of precious American blood; this destination was Omaha Beach. The salt water sprayed the men as they rode toward the beach in the small landing craft infantry (LCI). Their eyes saw firsthand a place that had so captured the attention of the world.[7]

By bus, by rail, by sea, by truck, by foot—Joe had never dreamed that he would ever travel so much. In fact, before the war he had never traveled outside of Kansas. Growing up, Joe's life had consisted of helping the family survive, not of seeing the world.

During the 1930s, the Great Depression raged throughout the United States and much of the world. Across the country, people searched for work, for anything that would put food on the table. In their western Kansas farm community, work was never something for which the Zimmerman family or their neighbors ever had to search. While it was incredibly hard to provide for the large family, they never went hungry. However, the farmers of the '30s had an additional problem that plagued them—the Dust Bowl. Years of improper farming and over-cultivation left the ground eroded and stripped of nutrients. Drought came, making the topsoil crumbly and fine, and as the ever-present winds blew, dust clouds formed, turning the brightest day into night.

The storms gave little warning. They came just in time to cancel a long-anticipated school picnic the Zimmerman kids and their schoolmates had prepared.[8] They came when people were at church. They came any time. People rushed home if they could find it; mothers covered the baby cribs and their children's mouths with wet cloths. The dust caused pneumonia and added work of shoveling dirt drifts and cleaning dirt-filled houses. Rosalie Zimmerman told her children she could always tell which direction the wind blew by the color of dirt the storm left—winds from the north brought Nebraska's black dirt while red dirt from Oklahoma remained after a southern wind.[9]

Not much grew during those years, and for a farmer, that was cause for concern. The kids picked weeds from the ditch to feed the hogs and chickens, or they herded the cattle to eat along the side of the road. "Hogs ate more weeds and rats than grain," remembered Fabian Zimmerman.

The family butchered their own meat, leaving absolutely nothing to waste. There was a use for everything from a hog's head to its feet, from its ears to its tail. They also ate an endless supply of rabbit. Jackrabbits severely overpopulated the area, so communities gathered for jackrabbit roundups. Adults and children walked across fields, herding hundreds of rabbits into a snow fence corral. Picking up a stick or club of some kind, they would then inflict a killing blow to the head while "rabbits would be screaming and carrying on." None were left alive as Fabian quickly learned. Once he noticed one little boy who had made friends with a particular rabbit during the roundup and wanted to take it home. A man walked up, grabbed the rabbit from the youngster and promptly killed it.

Everyone in the Zimmerman family worked hard together. After school the kids quickly changed clothes and grabbed a snack before bringing in and milking the cows and feeding the animals. They usually finished their work by 7:00 in the evening. A short time later in the next morning's predawn hours they woke up to again milk the thirty cows before school. To help the family even more, the older kids hired out to work, sometimes bringing home $1.50 as payment for a day's labor.[10] Everyone pitched in to survive. These were the kids who grew up to be the Greatest Generation.

———

Soon after reaching solid ground in France, Private Zimmerman crowded into the back of a truck for the cold, bumpy ride to the French/German border where the Allied forces were bogged down. The passing countryside was beautiful, many signs of war covered by snow. Finally, the convoy stopped at Sarreguemines, France, the first on a long list of French and German towns that Joe would "visit" as a foot soldier. For a few days, Joe waited at the replacement depot with thousands of seemingly nameless soldiers. They waited for their turn to be assigned to the front lines.

A man coming to the front lines in Europe in 1945 knew why he was there—some other guy "had got his." Unlike Germany and Britain, which withdrew entire divisions for rest and reinforcements, the United States dealt with the depletion of troops by sending a steady flow of individual men to the front. This strategy worked well as far as minimizing large-scale interruption, but for the replacements, it wreaked havoc. The army tore each man out of the security of a group (the buddies with whom he had trained or come overseas) and stuck him in a group of complete strangers. It stripped away all sense of community. The only commonalities for these soldiers were the uniform they wore and the fact that they were all alone together. One soldier spoke for the millions who experienced the replacement depot when he said, "Being a replacement is just like being an orphan. You are away from anybody you know and feel lost and lonesome." Although "replacements" were later called "reinforcements," the effect remained the same, and the system continued to be despised.[11]

The atmosphere hung thick with the reality of being so near the front lines. Although both armies had stopped fighting for the winter, a sense of military urgency hung in the air: final training and instructions, checking of equipment for the umpteenth time, meeting the man assigned to be your foxhole buddy, some final rest and, of course, endless waiting filled the days.[12]

As Joe sat at the replacement depot, commonly referred to as the "repple depple," he might have taken time to write letters to his family and to Martina. Sitting alone in the midst of hundreds of strangers, he surely thought of home.

———————

Home. Memories filled his mind, memories of his many brothers and sisters whom he loved to tease.[13] They had all spent hours playing together. Store-bought toys were nonexistent, but they had all learned how to make their own fun. "He was good at making things, building things for the kids. We could go down on a cart that he made, flying," said one twin sister, Albina.[14] Joe had made a coaster wagon the kids propelled with their feet and rode down the hills, and, without any sort of brakes, "flying" was a good term for the trip—if they did not crash along the way. Joe crafted other toys for his siblings. Stilts and hoops pushed with a stick gave them hours of fun. "If it weren't for the stuff he made, we would have had nothing to play with," recalled Johanna.[15]

The family treasured summer evenings and Sunday afternoons when they relaxed with extended family and neighbors. The kids played kick-the-can and baseball in the summer and fox-'n'-geese in the winter.[16] Participating in plays at the one-room Sunshine School also provided entertainment and much laughter. With so many family and friends around, one was rarely lonely.

———————

Time to move out! Joe officially became a member of the *63rd Infantry Division, 255th Regiment, L Company, 2nd Platoon.*

He and eighteen other men moved up to fill the recent vacancies in *Company L* in the Bliesbrucken Woods.[17] One seasoned veteran declared, "Boy, you were glad to see another guy come up, and, sometimes, were harsh with a newcomer, but…these were fellows that were pretty well trained by this time."[18] Some, and maybe most, veterans welcomed the new men, for they were desperately needed in battle. However, some veterans stayed away from and even looked down on the new guy in fear that he would panic in the midst of battle, thereby causing more harm on himself and others around him. Whether welcomed or shunned by the veterans, Joe and the other replacements quickly learned how to live on the front lines in order to not become the next casualty.[19] The games of basic training had become the harsh reality of war.

———————

The United States organized its Army Infantry into groups of threes. The entire United States Army was comprised of three army groups, and each army group was made up of three armies. Every army had three divisions (10,000-15,000 men), while a division had three infantry regiments (3,000-5,000 men). In a regiment there were three infantry battalions, which had three infantry rifle companies (62-190 men). Within a company existed three infantry rifle platoons (16-44 men), and every platoon had the most basic unit of three squads (9-10 men). However, no army is entirely made up of infantry, and each unit or group had its own support consisting of headquarters, artillery, medical, engineers and others.*

———

* For a detail of Joseph Zimmerman's infantry assignment, see Appendix A

As the commander of Supreme Headquarters Allied Expeditionary Force (Allied forces in Europe otherwise known as SHAEF), General Dwight Eisenhower had a straightforward yet tremendous task to accomplish—defeat the Germans as soon as possible. To do this, he looked to the three army groups under his command. The *Sixth Army Group* under Lieutenant General Jacob Devers held responsibility for southern France and Germany. Working under Devers were the three armies, the First French Army, General George Patton's Third Army and General Sandy Patch's *Seventh Army*. While General Patch was very successful with his *Seventh Army*, and, at times, more effective than General Patton, Patton's flamboyant nature commandeered everyone's attention. Often General Patch and the *Seventh Army* were relegated to the duty of supporting Patton.[20]

The men under General Patton's command had come to mainland Europe on June 6, 1944, (D-Day) through Operation Overlord. Lesser-known General Patch had also led an invasion of Europe that summer. In August, Operation Dragoon called for the *Seventh Army* to invade the southernmost French port in Marseilles. As Overlord forces had moved west through France, Dragoon forces had progressed north. On September 11, General Patton's Third Army had met General Patch's *Seventh Army*, thus securing General Eisenhower's strong line of invasion from Antwerp to the Swiss border.[21]

General Patch desperately needed men. Only two of the three divisions under his command had reached France, for the *63rd Division* (the division Zimmerman would join in 1945) was still in the States training and organizing its troops. Eventually, the decision was made that part of the *63rd* would go to Europe as Task Force Harris in November of 1944. They would assist as much as possible until the entire division joined.

Task Force Harris arrived in Europe at a critical time for

General Sandy Patch. The Allies were in the midst of fighting the Battle of the Bulge in the Ardennes Forest. Patton's men moved north as reinforcements, creating gaps in the defensive line as they transferred out. General Patch's units were constantly being moved to fill the newly emptied positions from Patton's army. On December 29, the *63rd Division's 255th Regiment* trucked through the freezing cold to support the 100th Division along the line.

New Year's Eve 1944 was picture perfect. A beautiful snow fell in the stillness; the rolling hills and thick woods portrayed a classic silent night. Even army-issued white coats covered the harsh reality of soldiers huddled in foxholes. While the world celebrated the new year, the Germans attacked.[22] As Joe enjoyed his last few days at home, Hitler began Operation Nordwind against the regiment that Joe would soon join.

The Battle of the Bulge had been raging for the last half of December, and it was not successful as Hitler had hoped. In a madman's attempt for victory, he decided to start a second two-pronged attack further south to split General Patch's *Seventh Army* and to stop them from sending reinforcements to Patton.[23] The Germans called this second assault Operation Nordwind (Northwind). In the next four days of heavy fighting, the eight German divisions advanced ten miles.[24]

As the Germans attacked around Lemberg, France, the 100th Division and the *63rd Division's 255th Regiment* fought with a fierce resistance. At the formation of the *63rd*, it had taken the name "Blood and Fire" in response to Winston Churchill's 1943 Casablanca speech stating the Allies would make the enemy "bleed and burn in expiation of their crimes against humanity."[25] In their first major conflict, the division proved themselves worthy of their name.

The soldiers battled in the true spirit of the "Blood and Fire," and some gave their all. As *L Company* retreated in the midst of one battle, Private First Class Maurice Lloyd continued to fight desperately with his Browning Automatic Rifle (BAR). Only later did the other men realize Lloyd had been shot, and a search for his body in the fresh blanket of snow proved fruitless. Over thirty years later in 1976, a French hiker discovered Private Lloyd's remains next to his rifle in a long-forgotten foxhole.[26]

Because of Private First Class Lloyd and thousands like him, the German's Operation Northwind was unsuccessful. As German activity lessened, the Allies began to retake the high ground and hold the line.

Everyday became much like the previous day: long, cold boredom interrupted by dangerous patrols and intermittent mortar and artillery fire. On January 25, Operation Northwind officially ended. The *Seventh Army* had suffered 11,609 battle casualties in the one month of fighting.[27]

CHAPTER FOUR

"There are no unwounded foxhole veterans."

Stephen E. Ambrose, *Citizen Soldiers*[1]

"Back in America the standard of living continued to rise. Back in America the race tracks were booming, the night clubs were making their greatest profits in history… [T]his [war] was a boom, this was prosperity, this was the way to fight a war. We read…and we wondered if the people would ever know what it cost the soldiers in terror, bloodshed, and hideous agonizing deaths to win the war."

Private David Webster[2]

Holding ground was the *255th Regiment's* job for the remainder of January. It sounded like a simple task—just sit still and don't move—but even "just" defending an area was not simple. As the Allied army slowly stretched out like a lumbering giant beginning to think about awaking from his winter's sleep, the men waited in their foxholes. The random explosions of German mortar and artillery fire, the long, boring days, the eerie quietness of night patrols into German controlled towns were all a part of the defenders' daily work.[3] And then there was the cold—always the cold. Men could not remember what it was like to not be cold. In their dreams they were cold. In their nightmares they were cold. As the most bitter winter in forty years, temperatures that month often dipped below zero; the ground froze; sleet pelted men's faces; heavy, wet snow made everything indistinguishable, a beautiful scene if it were not so cold.[4] A GI remembered, "One day we were moved three times and each time ordered to dig in. Dig in what? The ground was still frozen like concrete! Our overcoats that day were frozen stiff from the wet snow [sic] and ice on the roads made travel for we foot soldiers very difficult. When we would stop for a break we could stand our overcoats up they were so frozen."[5]

By February 1, the remaining elements of the *63rd Division* arrived from the States and joined the *255th Regiment* and the rest of Task Force Harris.[6] General Alexander "Sandy" Patch finally had a full Army of three divisions with which to work. After arriving, the *63rd Division* headquartered in Sarreguemines, France, and filled empty positions with any available replacements in preparation for its upcoming attack on the Bliesbrucken Woods.

Ideally, an infantry regiment in 1945 totaled approximately 3,000 men. Three thousand individuals, each with his own personality, fears, and expectations, worked together to help accomplish a great feat in history, defeating the Nazi's Third Reich. Within that one regiment, there were a few soldiers who neglected their duty or ran from the terror (and, in all honesty, no one can say until faced with the same situation that he would not do the same). However, most bravely faced tortuous maiming or death. Some members of the regiment later lived with fame and fortune. One such man was Anthony Benedetto of Company G who spent some free time as the vocalist in the *255th Regimental Band*. But in war, Benedetto, or Tony Bennett as he was later known, was no better than the next guy; the next guy was no different than Benedetto. They all did what they had to; they all tried to make it through alive, knowing no guarantee of survival. War is one of the greatest equalizers—it has no favorites.

After successfully taking the Bliesbrucken Woods by February 16, Private Zimmerman settled in with *Company L* into defensive positions. As often as possible, the mess hall sent forward welcome hot breakfasts in the early morning darkness.[7] Around 6:00 a.m., men appeared out of the snowy ground. Boots crunched slowly across the snow and arms swung wide as the dark, bulky forms, clothed with every available piece of winter gear, worked to extend their cramped limbs. Quiet scraping and the muffled clatter of mess kits, hushed talking, a chuckle here and there, feet occasionally stamping to get the blood flowing were probably the only human sounds in the dark, snowy woods. They had a few minutes—that was all—a few minutes to move around and visit with the other men. As light came to the sky, they trudged in separate directions and disappeared back into their foxholes.[8] At 5' 6½", Joe was not a tall man and could fit better than most into the 3 foot by 6 foot hole that he shared with another soldier. However, "fitting better than most" still did not mean fitting comfortably. As tight as that space might have been, the GIs still preferred it to the German shelling brought about by any movement above ground.

Foxhole buddies were assigned, not chosen. Whether a soldier loved or hated his buddy, he certainly knew him better than anyone else. He knew his family, his girlfriend or wife, his childhood memories, his dreams and fears; he knew him well. Since each hole was anywhere from a few yards to a hundred yards apart, most conversation could only be held with the other man in the 6 foot long by 3 foot wide by 5 foot deep hole. Having everything familiar stripped away from them and being thrown into intense danger drew the men closely together in a unique brotherhood. Many times, the connection between foxhole buddies developed into the closest, most open relationship they had or would ever have.[9] As the days warmed and the melting snow trickled into the hole, as the Blies River rushed by in the distance and occasional artillery shells exploded, Joe and his buddy talked or silently thought of home.[10]

The winter night fell by 4:45 p.m., and around 6:00 p.m. men once again moved toward the promise of a hot meal and a quick conversation before having to endure an additional twelve hours of silent, boring darkness. As temperatures dropped each night, turning the rain and melting snow to ice, men worked to keep their weapons and feet from freezing. That winter, soldiers constantly battled trench foot, an enemy that caused almost as many casualties as did fighting the Germans. With the constant cold and wet conditions, socks and boots were perpetually soggy, causing the feet to rot. Almost every day, *Company L* sent men back to the medical battalion because of their feet.[11] Those who did not succumb to the dreaded trench foot had mastered some sort of system to dry their socks. Many times they kept the extra pair under their shirts to keep the socks from freezing and allow them time to dry.

On the front lines during World War II, the coming of night did not bring the promise of rest. The Germans shelled the American positions they had observed during the day, having mastered the art of firing artillery into the tree tops so spears of wood joined shrapnel on its deadly mission. Although the men took precautions of covering their foxholes with what tree branches they could find, this did not guarantee their protection. Stephen Ambrose recreates the experience as he wrote, "Cries of 'Medic!' Tree limbs hurtling through the air. The smell of powder. The bangs and flashes and booms and screams, red-hot bits of metal zooming through the air. The only movement you could make was to press ever closer to the ground. Those who endured such a cataclysm were forever scarred by it, even if untouched by shrapnel."[12]

Having endured such shellings, Private Arnold Parish recalled his thoughts. "We were helpless and all alone and there was nothing we could do, so I prayed to God...The time went by very slow. I tried to keep warm but that wasn't possible. I thought about my mother and hoped she didn't know where I was or what I was doing...Maybe this is the end of the world, I thought."[13]

When not under fire, the darkness gave the men opportunity to restring communication lines or concertina wire and to repair foxholes. Also, each night an officer selected men to guard the outpost position even farther to the front and nervously watch for German patrols. Often the Americans conducted their own dreaded night patrols to find and silence the German mortar and artillery fire, to capture a prisoner for information or simply to cause a disruption behind the enemy lines. A GI remembered, "One night patrol is just like another. The sense of uneasiness before you start, the slight, gnawing anxiety as you set out... an anxiety you don't quite admit...The terrain was wooded and difficult or open and dangerous...Maybe you were supposed to bring back a prisoner, maybe only to look and listen to find where the enemy was…But you didn't like patrols…It was the kind of stuff that takes the heart out of you…" With so much work, men on the front lines managed to snatch an average of two to four hours of interrupted sleep each night. The GI's description of the front lines continued with the winter conditions the men endured, "This, then, was the locale for the long boredom of winter warfare. The endless cold and misery of foxholes, trench foot and nervous kidneys. The routine shift from foxholes to reserve positions in crowded, smoky houses. The reluctant shift back to the foxholes again—foxholes that we logged over, and propped up and floored under until they took on the aspect of permanent habitations."[14]

Actually, Joe had stayed awake through the night on many occasions at home. The Depression made life difficult for families, but it also taught many lessons to individuals. Ted and Rosalie Zimmerman expected their children to work on the farm and go to school (at least until eighth grade). Milking the cows before dawn and again after dusk and working or going to school in between, the kids did not have the luxury of extra personal time, except at night.

Always one to create a business venture for personal cash, especially combined with his love of hunting, Joe decided he would sell animal hides. As night fell, he and his brother Fabian hunted anything from bobcats to rabbits, primarily targeting skunks. Finding one of the black and white creatures waddling through the darkness, they caught it and beat it on the head—only after the skunk had imparted his final revenge. By morning, the boys sometimes came home with ten to fifteen skunks and an odor that could be smelled in the next county. But at $12.50 per hide, they didn't much care.[15]

―――――――――

In 1945, warm weather came suddenly and quickly melted the snow. This brought on a new set of challenges for the army. Water and mud now ran into foxholes and also further impeded troop and vehicle movement. Historian Ken Hechler noted that the weather "was cold, clammy and rainy. Sweat mixed with grime and underwear stuck and stank."[16] Even worse was that the melting snow sometimes revealed bodies of soldiers killed and lost during the winter battles making burial detail a more common task.[17]

In the afternoon of February 27, *Love Company* moved back to division headquarters in Sarreguemines, France, for one day of rest.[18] With several weeks' worth of mud and sweat caked on, Zimmerman and the other soldiers entered the relative safety of town for a much-needed bath, fresh clothes and a little sleep. First Lieutenant Jack Kerins of D Company said, "We were brought back a little ways, given two seconds for soaping and a three second rinse and fresh clothes. Was it good to get out of those smelly and muddy clothes and feel clean again. It was our first bath in almost a month except for our own helmet sponges while on the line."[19] The men were quartered in Steinbacher Hof, once a mental institution with broken windows and no furniture, but who cared? It was relatively warm, dry and clean compared to the foxholes.[20]

During both the German and Allied occupations, the Sarreguemines had suffered little damage.[21] It sat on a beautiful location in the middle of the plains of Alsace, the Saar River running through the middle, the Blies River circling partway around the outskirts. Situated on the border of France and Germany, the

Alsatian plains had a long history of battle as both countries had alternately claimed the area.

————————

    As the weather warmed, the soldiers could once again believe in the faint promise of spring. But with spring also came another promise—the Allied invasion of Germany. Through the morning of March 1, the *3rd Battalion* moved back to the front lines at Wiesinger Hof, France, to relieve the 1st Battalion so it could prepare to attack the Germans who held the high ground.[22] Private Zimmerman found an abandoned foxhole and crawled in for the familiar waiting and watching for the enemy. That night, he sat, pen in hand, and escaped to another world, a future world he hoped to share with his sweetheart.

"I Love You"

I love you dear with all my heart,
And I never was sorry from the very start.
I hope to come back to you some day,
And this time I hope it's forever to stay.

I'm glad that soon I can call you my wife,
To live with you a happy life.
We'll live on a farm all our own,
A place we can call our home sweet home.

As I sit here tonight I think of you dear
And I wish so much that you could be here.
I would hold you tight, and kiss you again,
I'm sure it would be like the first night we began.

At night when I go to bed you are in my dreams
You are so close it always seems
I want you to know as I say So long
Darling to me you will always belong

J.T.Z.—March 1, 1945[23]

The *255th Regiment* was involved in three different battles the beginning of that March to prepare for the upcoming invasion. One such brutal fight became known as the Battle of the Quarry, fought by the 253rd Regiment and the 1st Battalion of the *255th Regiment*. Scrambling up the rocky slopes, the men eventually won the high ground, but suffered many casualties.[24]

The eleven days at Wiesinger Hof, *Company L* reported the usual few cases of trench foot and sickness. One enlisted man was killed in action, and two others went AWOL one morning. Replacements came; men were promoted. Life carried on as normally as the front lines allowed. First Lieutenant Robert Brice noted on March 10, "*Company [L]* [italics added] in reserve... receiving two hot meals per day. Sleeping quarters good. Morale excellent." Arriving shortly before midnight on March 12, *Company L* returned to Sarreguemines, a town crowded with soldiers.[25] In addition to a bath and warm sleeping quarters, the men received lighter gear and leather combat boots to replace their winter shoepacks.[26] For two days they rested, wrote letters home, cleaned equipment, received replacements and trained how to attack a fortification.[27] The high ground had been won; now the Siegfried Line waited.

CHAPTER FIVE

"We were still all scared but now we were veterans.
But I don't think any of us ever got over being scared."

First Lieutenant Jack Kerins[1]

"[T]here was no way training could prepare a man for combat.
Combat could only be experienced, not played at. Training was
critical to getting the men into physical condition to obey orders,
to use their weapons, to work effectively with hand signals and
radios and more. It could not teach men how to lie helpless under
a shower of shrapnel in a field crisscrossed by machine-gun fire.
They just had to do it, and in doing it they joined a unique group
of men who have experienced what the rest of us cannot imagine."

Stephen Ambrose, *Citizen Soldiers*[2]

The battles fought by the fathers and uncles of these soldiers
during the First World War had been vicious and involved over-

whelming bloodshed. Both sides had built an intricate maze of trenches in which they stayed for days, weeks, months at a time. Enemy faced enemy, but, in this war, each enemy lived below ground. The atrocity occurred when the men were ordered to attack. Soldiers advanced in mass groups, an outmoded strategy used sixty years previous during the American Civil War. Walking toward the enemy into rifle and canon fire was fiercely gruesome; walking toward the enemy into machine gun and artillery fire was appalling and senseless. A "normal" war scars her warriors; World War I brutalized hers.

Traumatized from trench warfare, by the 1920s European nations looked at the possibility of building vast, "impregnable" walls of fortification (souped-up trenches) to ward off attacks into their land. World War I veteran Andre Maginot conceived an idea for such a defense on France's eastern border, and by 1929 construction on the Maginot Line began. Of course, the Germans also wished to build a wall on their border opposing the Maginot Line. However, the victors distrusted the vanquished, and the Treaty of Versailles ending World War I withheld the German's right to build such a wall. As the French constructed their imposing line of defense, the Germans assembled a collection of minor, scattered forts.

The year of 1929 was significant for another reason—economic depression swept across the American and European nations. Times became terribly difficult in the United States but horrific in Germany. Saddled in 1919 with a war debt they could never hope to repay, the German people sank to a point of hopelessness by 1923. Inflation rose uncontrollably to a point, according to well-circulated stories, that people used wheelbarrows full of money to buy one loaf of bread—that is, if they owned wheelbarrows full of money. Most did not. At the end of the First World War, one dollar had equaled 4.2 German marks; five years later, 4.2 *million* German marks bought one dollar. Under a new plan in 1924 in which Germany received loans from other countries (primarily the United States), the highly volatile government finally stabilized. But as the United States economy crashed in 1929, the German economy declined even further.[3]

In such a state of despair, Germans found hope in the leader of the rising National Socialist Worker's Party. Adolf Hitler promised to bring a strong sense of pride back to the people—pride in themselves and, more importantly, pride in their country. While the group and its ideas were not new, the Nazi party grew practically overnight in the fall of 1930 as intense German nationalism revitalized throughout the country.[4] In less than a decade, one man, one political party and millions of people transformed from a defeated, weak, depressed country into one of the most powerful and successful nations of that day.

This intense nationalism transferred to the building of fortifications on the Franco-German border. The German government wanted to protect the country, so in 1934, it answered the French Maginot Line challenge and began to transform its minor forts into a similarly fortified wall. Named after the designer, this continuous line of defense along the entire border shared with France became known as the Siegfried Line.

———————————

As the Allies rushed across France in 1944, they found two kinds of German soldiers. The first was the type who did not want to fight. They never believed in the Nazi cause, or they realistically knew Germany had already lost the war, or they trusted the Americans more than the Russians approaching from the eastern front, or they were just plain scared and tired of war. Many times these soldiers were old men, young boys, or men from conquered countries forced to fight for Germany. Whoever they were and whatever their reasons, they surrendered to the American Army, sometimes one or two at a time and sometimes en masse.

The second type fought past all hope of victory before retreating to fight another day. Many of these men were Hitler's SS troops, the elite forces. These were the soldiers who fell back to the Siegfried Line in the latter part of 1944 to make penetration of the German border as difficult and costly as possible.

As Private Zimmerman and thousands of men in Eisenhower's Allied Army approached the Siegfried Line in March, 1945, they faced a formidable obstacle. Rolls of upon rolls of barbed wire and thousands of schu-mines stretched out before the wall. Just past the mine fields sat hundreds of dragon's teeth, interspersed with more land mines. Dragon's teeth were comprised of three rows of concrete pyramids three feet high and buried three feet deep and were staggered in such a way that tanks could not go around, over or through them. When men or tanks did manage to penetrate the line of dragon's teeth, they then faced ditches twelve feet wide and eight feet deep. One mile behind the barrier of wire, mines, dragon's teeth and ditches came another line exactly the same. Behind these two extensive barricades, the invaders finally came to the Siegfried Line, which consisted of five hundred yards of concrete bunkers or "pillboxes."

The location and construction of pillboxes varied widely. Some sat openly on the top of hills; some hid in the woods, camouflaged so well with earth and vegetation that they were invisible until a soldier was almost on top of them. Some served as underground cities complete with kitchens, infirmaries and barracks that could support a hundred men. Others consisted of concrete rooms that could hold only fifteen defenders. No matter the location or the size, pillboxes were situated in such a way that defenders in one bunker could cover the approach to another bunker. However, just as the Civil War tactic of advancing in groups toward the enemy was obsolete in World War I, the World War I tactic of building a static line of defense was outmoded in World War II. Weapons had advanced, and no matter how strong the forts might have felt, they actually confined the German soldiers. Large guns could not fit into them; the construction limited movement; and they posed as fair game for massive artillery fire.[5] The Siegfried Line was difficult and dangerous to attack, but it was *not* impregnable.

By March 14, the men felt high anticipation of impending battle. While generals did not tell privates detailed plans, the privates saw the obvious situation. Weather had warmed; troops were gathered and given clean, lighter equipment and trained for night attacks on pillboxes; and the Siegfried Line lay a few miles away. Operation Undertone called for General Patton and his Third Army to attack from the north while General Patch and his *Seventh Army* attacked from the south. Once they broke through the barrier, the armies would meet and move together across Germany. General Louis Hibbs, commanding officer of the *63rd Division*, wrote a directive to be read to his men.

Last month this Division brilliantly forced the crossing of the Saar River and led the *Seventh Army* [italics added] onto German soil. Before tomorrow the *Seventh Army* [italics added] attacks along the entire front. In the coming attack, you will again strike first, into and through the Siegfried Line—blasting a hole in the enemy's vaunted West Wall, last barrier to the Rhine.[6]

Men of the *255th Regiment* moved out of Sarreguemines and waited at the Saar River. Finally, at 8:15 p.m. on March 14, *L Company* began to ferry across the rushing water, and, two hours later, arrived in the *255th's* staging area in the Mühlenwald (forest).[7] Perhaps Joe looked through the midnight darkness and saw the flickering light of a French home in a quiet valley or a German farm on a distant hill.[8] Perhaps he thought of home. Perhaps the upcoming battle and his possible death filled his mind. Once *Company L* reached the dense woods, soldiers dug their foxholes and crawled in for some rest. The night was pitch black and tense with anticipation.[9]

At 1:00 a.m. the night erupted; floodlights illuminated the inky sky; artillery exploded. The Allies began the battle for the Siegfried Line. Kerins of D Company recalled, "Now we looked forward to a little rest before daylight. Suddenly right before our eyes began the most dazzling display of artillery fire that any of us had ever seen. Shells from our artillery, tanks and mortars opened up with a deafening roar as our weaponry poured shell after shell into and onto the Siegfried fortifications…the noise was so deafening you couldn't hear the fellows in the next foxhole."[10] Colonel Hatcher stated, "At the appointed moment great flashes rent the black of night and the midnight sky danced with the licking flames of blasts from hundreds of guns deployed back of our lines…"[11] For two hours, the Allies barraged the German troops in an attempt to shock them before the infantry attacked. The German artillery answered with a defiant response.

The night's artillery battle soon turned into the day's infantry battle, and as the sun steadily rose behind them, Kerins saw that the "[d]aylight now gave us a ringside view of our frontage. There in full view was the most formidable and supposedly impregnable fortress in the world."[12] P-39 Lightnings and P-47 Thunderbolts zoomed overhead, dropping their bomb load onto the fortified Germans.[13]

As artillery shells screamed overhead, *Company L* moved out. Men stumbled over the difficult terrain, pushed through thick trees, and scrambled up slopes and down ditches.[14] Behind them came the whining of tanks; in front of them continued the explosions of a thousand shells; around them came the grunting and curses of fellow soldiers.[15] Throughout the morning, line after line of troops moved across the countryside, each soldier seeing little more than the few men immediately surrounding him but feeling the mighty force of the powerful Allied Army.

Through the German artillery and mortar fire, across mine fields, around machine gun and small arms fire, the *255th Regiment* advanced toward the battle line. Some units quickly reached their objective—the *3rd Battalion*, led by K Company and supported by their own mortar team, took only seventeen minutes to claim the wooded hill east of Bliesransbach. Private Paul Winkler, fellow member of Zimmerman in the *2nd Platoon*, recalled coming across German bodies in the forest. The memory stuck with him, and he emphatically stated sixty-five years later that "it was not a pleasant sight."[16] Across the valley, the 2nd Battalion met staunch resistance, fighting for several costly hours to reach their assigned area.[17]

Moving along the road, Joe and his fellow troops experienced the cautiousness of advancing through open terrain, the comfort of nearby tank and artillery support, the dread of approaching the next objective, and the thrill of victory. Through the Saarbach Valley from Bliesransbach to Eschringen, from Eschringen to Ensheim, from hill to valley, from valley to wooded hill they fought.[18] For their noon "meal," they dug out their chocolate D bar as they moved along.[19] Once it reached a wooded rise near Kirkelbach that afternoon, the *3rd Battalion* experienced heavy enemy machine gun, mortar, artillery and self-propelled rocket fire. That day, Winkler went over a hill before being shot.[20] Picking their way through a minefield, the Americans managed to finally outflank and silence the enemy's guns. By 5:00 p.m., the men had fought nine hours, captured eighty prisoners, overrun several 150mm and 80mm guns and advanced five miles.[21] That night, the battle-weary GIs feasted on K-rations.[22]

The regiment continued to move closer to the Siegfried Line the next couple of days. It feinted an attack northwest of Ommersheim to give the 254th Regiment an opportunity to launch a heavier offensive toward the southwest.[23] Both feinted attacks and main attacks had the same results for the foot soldier. *Love Company* lost at least nine percent of their forces on March 16 alone, reporting ten men wounded in action and seven missing. At this point very few replacements were being sent forward.[24]

At 5:30 a.m. on March 17, *Companies L* and K marched through the pre-dawn light followed by tanks and the protective tank destroyer battalions. They moved unopposed to the high ground southwest of Hecken-Dahlheim, Germany, and began to dig in by 6:17 a.m. As the sun rose, sniper, machine gun and mortar fire rained down. By 10:00 a.m., the 255th's supporting tanks fired on the Siegfried Line and men of the 1st and 2nd Battalions attacked through the smoke and dust, capturing a few pillboxes by the end of the next day.[25] The fight against the West Wall defenders was harder than the battles of the previous winter.[26] Sometimes it required hand to hand combat, but the soldiers slowly made progress.[27]

The 254th and *255th Regiments* continued to attack through the next day. Engineers blew a path through the dragon's teeth to allow a continued advance. Choking dust rose. Tank gears ground. Machine guns popped. Artillery deafened. Wounded men screamed for help. Medics shielded by small red crosses on their armbands rushed to answer their pleas. Under covering fire, groups of two or three men ran forward to insert Bangalore torpedoes into the pillbox vents. During the assault, the *3rd Battalion* held a defensive position. Zimmerman hunkered down in his foxhole as the too-familiar, high-pitched sounds of German rockets known as "Screaming Mimis" flew through the air.[28]

The sixth and final day of fighting against the Siegfried Line dawned on March 20. *Company L* moved forward with the *3rd Battalion* on the road toward Hassel to make the final push. The 254th Regiment made the first penetration of the "impenetrable" Siegfried Line. Shortly after, the *255th Regiment* punched a hole near Nieder-Wurzbach.[29] The fighting had been long and fierce, but Germany's last bastion had fallen. Soon a sign went up proclaiming to all who followed, "You're passing through the Siegfried Line, courtesy of the *63rd Infantry Division* [italics added]."[30] In all of the *Seventh Army*, these two regiments were first in accomplishing the mission.[31]

Major General Hibbs commended his men.

My congratulations, Hot Shots! You broke into and through the Siegfried Line and turned loose the armor into Germany! This was your immediate mission. Add another glorious page to the history of this your *63rd Blood and Fire Infantry Division* [italics added].[32]

Operation Undertone was completed. General Patch's *Seventh Army* met General Patton's Third Army, and together they invaded toward the Rhine River and into the heart of the Nazi Fatherland.

CHAPTER SIX

"An infantryman has to fashion means for his comfort. He has to resort to expediencies to ameliorate some of the harshness of field living for he becomes filthy by tramping for days without washing; his hair becomes matted, dirty and stiff with the constant wearing of the metal helmet, and as he tries to comb it, it falls in tufts, and his scalp pains to the touch. He picks up ticks, fleas, and body lice from sleeping in hay stacks, on open fields, holes in the ground, with animals in barns, and in demolished, filth-spewed hovels. And he just might conceive, as we once did, of dousing his clothes and body with gasoline in order to rid himself of lice."

Ralph M. Morales, rifleman, 254th Infantry Regiment[1]

Throughout the spring of 1945, the Americans and British invaded western Germany, while the Russians attacked from the east. Each side, allies by necessity but enemies by nature, raced each other to reach Berlin first. However, General Eisenhower, realizing the futility of trying to beat Russia to the capital, turned his focus to southern Germany. The *Sixth Army Group*, including Patch's *Seventh Army* and Patton's Third Army, answered Eisenhower's order and moved quickly toward the Bavarian Alps. There remained a high possibility that Hitler would make a costly last stand in his mountain stronghold in the south. Besides that, ghastly rumors began to spread of a thing called concentration camps in the area. Hitler had to be crushed, and the innocent victims had to be rescued.[2]

The morning of March 21, the smell of a hot breakfast, the first real meal in several days, wafted through the air.[3] Battle-weary men gathered as a small community, bonded not only by a common location but also by the shared horrors of war. Lieutenant John Brown recalled life on the front lines as "[s]ometimes pretty awful, if not brutal; other times just dirty, nasty. People didn't get a chance to get a bath for weeks on end, or shave…Everybody learned to take a bath in a helmet full of water, meaning you just splash your face sometimes." He did note though that "it wasn't endless days and nights of absolute groveling in the dirt."[4] Weary shoulders might have sagged a little that morning, or high spirits from the recent victory may have prevailed. Either way, the men faced a new day, and they had little time for reflection.

By 8:00 a.m., *Love Company*, under the command of Lieutenant Cecil Johnson, left its location a half mile northeast of Triebsdierdor, and the men marched twenty miles in six hours on the road to Homburg.[5] Along the way, they found large numbers of passive Italian and Russian troops who had been pressed into service in the German Army.[6] The American troops also met French civilians traveling back toward their home with livestock and wagons loaded with loot from German towns overrun by the French troops. As human nature goes, to the victor belongs the spoils, and the French were clearly enjoying their newfound status. However, for the men of the United States Army, this was not the case. Looting of civilians was strictly prohibited though enemy troops were considered fair game. At one point, an officer lined up the men of the *255th's* Company B to allow a German woman the opportunity to look for a soldier she accused of stealing her rings. This army was fighting for a cause bigger than loot.[7]

Arriving in Homburg, the foot soldiers were exhausted, dirty and jumpy from the recent battle and march. The weary men gratefully received the unexpected privilege of sleeping quarters in houses that night.[8] As they slept, a sentry shot an approaching officer who did not hear, and therefore did not answer, the challenge call. Because of inexperience and nervousness, *255th Regiment* lost a valuable leader.[9]

The next day, Zimmerman climbed into a truck and rode a short distance to Limbach where the company rested, cleaned equipment, received thirteen much-needed replacements and waited for orders. Some of the men now joining the *255th* had recently been pulled from the Air Force Pilot Training Program to fill the empty infantry ranks. They did not receive their new infantry assignment well.[10]

On March 24, the men once again began the move toward the Rhine River. From Limbach to Beeden they walked, warmed by the afternoon sun. From Beeden to Höringen they rode, chilled by the midnight air.[11] The faint lights and pungent smell of cigarettes filled the area under the truck canvas. The rumbling diesel motors and grinding truck gears banished the silence.

———

Huddling under the canvas of the truck in the cold might have reminded Private Zimmerman of similar times growing up. After milking cows and eating breakfast each winter morning, the Zimmerman kids hurriedly crowded into the buggy for the ride to their one-room schoolhouse. Once on the road, Joe quickly secured the reins of the well-trained horse and crawled under the heavy quilts with the other kids.[12] One morning in the barn at school, Joe did not immediately remove the horse's bridle. The horse stepped on the rein and broke it, making it far too short to tie to the buggy on the way home. He had to reach far out in front of him all the way home in the bitter cold just to hold that broken rein.[13]

Riding across Germany, Joe looked around as he sat in the back of the truck. Instead of brothers and sisters, he saw wartime buddies; instead of the warm breath of kids, he breathed stale smoke; instead of the *clip-clop* of horse hooves, he heard the crunch of tires; and, in the distance, instead of the ringing of the school bell, he anticipated the distant, muffled *whump* of artillery explosions.

———————

March 28, *Company L* dug in near the Rhine River and waited for the engineers to complete the new pontoon bridge at Worms, Germany. Distant sounds of battle came from the south, but having been placed in reserve behind the advancing forces, the *63rd Division* enjoyed a moment of relative quiet.[14] Finally, as darkness came, they loaded into trucks and crossed the last major barrier in Germany.[15]

The day's good weather turned cold, and rain began to fall. The men unloaded at Lorscher Wald (forest) a few miles north of Mannheim and moved a little way from the autobahn to dig foxholes for the night. The supply trucks carrying blankets and the field kitchen were still stuck on the other side of the river, so Joe opened K-rations or munched on a chocolate D-bar before settling in for a cold, wet night. Despite the miserable conditions, Colonel Hatcher wrote of that night, "As I moved from company to company and observed the cheerfulness of the men under these adverse circumstances, my own opinion of the fighting spirit of the regiment I then commanded caused me to feel most humble in my new assignment."[16]

The boredom of the miserable night did not last long, for by 3:00 a.m. on March 29, *Company L* moved out of the woods toward the historic city of Heidelberg.[17] They arrived north of the city at Schriesheim by 5:00 a.m. and relieved the 44th Infantry Division's 3rd Battalion, and waited to attack the city the next morning.[18]

After climbing the steep, narrow road, the men rested in houses overlooking the Neckar River. Sharp hills surrounded *Company L's* location; some were covered in thick woods, and others were filled to the edge of the river with vineyards. Zimmerman had little opportunity to appreciate the beauty of the city as snipers intermittently fired on the men, but at some point, he might have been able to see "the blown out spans of that beautiful stone bridge" like D Company's Lieutenant Kerins.[19] The medieval city centered around the ancient Heidelberg Castle and Heidelberg University built in 1386. Since the Allies had respected the Heidelberg's historic value, it remained almost untouched by devastating effects of wartime bombing. At the foot of the hills, the old village gave way to a newer, modern city of eighty-five thousand people.[20] Weeks later as the 101st Airborne Division moved through, Private David Webster noted, "When we saw all the undamaged buildings and the beautiful river promenade, where complacent civilians strolled in the sun, I was ready to stay in Heidelberg forever. The green hills, the warm sunlight, the cool, inviting river, the mellow collegiate atmosphere—Heidelberg spelled paradise in any language."[21]

March 30, the *63rd Division* prepared for attack. The *3rd Bat-*

talion left at 4:30 a.m. and moved south along the highway toward the city. The plan was to have Companies I and K move forward while *Company L* would "move by stealth, in column of twos with scouts close in, along the mountain side east of Schrieshiem [*sic*] and Dossenhiem [*sic*]." Colonel Hatcher continued to recount that he felt "[t]he attempt to infiltrate a company to the rear of Dossenheim was extremely hazardous business" since the enemy could cut off the invasion force from the rest of the battalion. The solemnity of impending battle hung thick as the men marched through the cool, dark morning. "Tense hours passed" for Hatcher, and slowly "the anxious hours drew toward daybreak and time for the five minute artillery preparation preceding the regimental assault approached." Headquarters had lost all communication with *Company L*.[22] At 6:26 a.m., as the sun rose, the men attacked. Besides coming across large amounts of wire, they actually met little resistance and were quickly able to overrun the German artillery positions and capture many prisoners without giving them opportunity to fall back.[23] Private Zimmerman and his company had accomplished their mission to secure "the high ground northeast of the bridge site on the main road across the Neckar from old Heidelberg."[24]

Company I joined *Love Company*, and they quickly pressed toward the bridges in Heidelberg's Neuenheim subdivision, only to find them completely destroyed by the time they arrived at 8:10 a.m. Gathering canoes and rowboats from nearby sheds, the soldiers crossed under light artillery fire from the fast-retreating Germans. Once across, Zimmerman's company moved swiftly south through the city along Römerstrasse (Römer Street) meeting only pockets of gunfire.[25] Before any heavy bombardment of the city began, Heidelberg's Bürgermeister (mayor) contacted the *3rd Battalion's* commanding officer and declared it an open city. Heidelberg would remain virtually untouched by the war.[26]

In the defeated city, civilians came out of their houses to see the Americans. They were not welcoming, neither were they resistant.[27] The *255th Regiment's 3rd Battalion* took eighty-one German prisoners including Nazi scientist, General Major Ernst Rodenwaldt.[28] However, many German soldiers escaped by quickly retreating or changing into civilian clothes and melting into the population.[29]

Early the next morning, *L Company* mounted on tanks and tank destroyers and moved toward the next objective in yet another German city.[30] As the sun rose that Easter morning, Joe must have thought of home and family. Kerins in D Company recalled, "It was a perfect day, not a cloud in the sky, and not a sound of war."[31]

CHAPTER SEVEN

"He [the infantryman] should be taught to fight a violent, relentless but honorable battle. He lives and fights in the presence of extreme violence and death and his own courage and self-sacrifice is enhanced by the knowledge that his conscience is clear; that he is prepared to kill human beings in the performance of his duty and in the defense of comrades and his ideals; but that such duty is performed without malice and with no criminal impulse."

Colonel James E. Hatcher[1]

Both of the attacking battalions [2nd Battalion and *3rd Battalion*] were to be reinforced with tank, tank destroyer, and assault gun elements and were to attack with all speed and violence along roads between enemy strongpoints, using reconnaissance to seek out and destroy organized enemy resistance in the intervals between the lines of communication. The attack hour was 0900A [9:00 a.m.] 1 April 1945.[2] — Field Order Number 4

The men of *Love Company* held on to their uncomfortable seats the best they could as the tanks rumbled through a valley southeast of Heidelberg.[3] While his brothers and sisters hunted for Easter baskets that morning, Zimmerman hunted for Germans. Riding atop a tank, he might have remembered sunny Easters of the past. The tanks' whining and grinding noise might have faded a bit as he dreamed of a home-cooked meal like the one his family was enjoying. Did he think of egg hunts and Easter morning mass? Did he recall the time he switched candy for dried cow pies in his siblings' Easter baskets?[4] Maybe. Or maybe in the midst of war he forgot that it was Easter at all.

By 10:00 that clear morning, *Company L* had already successfully fought for and taken their first objective at Maisbach. They advanced cautiously through the valley toward Schatthausen, a sparkling stream meandering along the way, while the engineering battalion led to clear the roads of minefields. Suddenly the enemy from the hills above opened up small arms fire, and Zimmerman and his buddies dove for cover. Pinned down for a time by the flying bullets, *Love* eventually overcame the Germans and continued east, this time on foot.[5]

At 3:00 p.m., *L Company* neared Unterhof, their final objective for the day. One hundred twenty-five German troops supported by a few tanks and half-tracks defended the town and offered such resistance that the company had to fight for a couple hours.[6] The men struggled as enemy tanks continued the barrage. Colonel Hatcher recorded, "Repeated calls…for fire on these tanks was unavailing, and the distress calls from the *3rd Battalion* [italics added] became more and more pressing."[7] Hatcher's decision to give the company the required support aided them in beating back the enemy and taking Unterhof by 5:00 p.m.[8]

Company L stopped for the night, and the men automatically began to dig foxholes. Anderson of the 1st Battalion wrote, "Our supper caught up to us that night and, as a bonus, the jeep was towing a trailer loaded with blankets. After digging in we were able to use the blankets to keep warm…It was really appreciated by all."[9] That day, the *3rd Battalion*—Companies I, K and *L*— had advanced sixteen miles in eleven hours. They had overcome stiff resistance and captured 170 enlisted men and 3 officers, at the cost of 4 killed and 16 wounded in action.[10] The men were exhausted, but Private Zimmerman's work was not over.

Growing up as the son of German immigrants, Joe Zimmerman primarily spoke German until he reached school age. Entering the one-room schoolhouse as a young child, Joe looked around at the other kids. Many of them would become friends, some of them would insist on teasing. "Russian!" a classmate called out to Joe's sister Mary. Mary quickly reached out and slapped the classmate across the face. With a glare of hate, the girl grabbed Mary's writing tablet and tore it up in front of her. Thankfully, the teacher did not allow such nonsense, and the girl had to buy Mary a new tablet, but the thought behind the act was still there.[11]

Most people in the western Kansas community had come to trust and respect their German neighbors, but there were a few families who could not look past the differences. The same situation followed Joe into the army—many of the men accepted and liked him. Terrell Wright in *Love Company's 2nd Platoon* said, "I thought a whole lot of Zimmerman, a real nice sort of fellow, agreeable and pleasant. We got along."[12] However, there were those who distrusted Joe because of his German heritage. According to his sister Alberta, some men wondered if he was really an American soldier or a spy for the enemy.[13]

His sister Johanna recalled the conversation when her brother told the family, "They wanted to know who could speak German, so I said I could." His dad, wiser in the army ways, replied, "You should have never said that."[14] Whether or not he should have volunteered the information, whether or not he was sorry he had, the officers of *Company L* appointed Zimmerman as one of their interpreters. Joe's brother Eddie proudly recalled that "he would fight in the day and interpret [for German prisoners] at night."[15]

Late into the night…"What unit are you from from? "How many Germans are in the area?" "Where is your artillery located?"…questions and more questions. With many prisoners, Joe easily obtained answers. As Colonel Hatcher noted, "Naturally a newly captured soldier is by no means sure that his life is safe and there is a strong urge to curry favor with his captors by giving them what information he can. German soldiers are by habit and training particularly amenable to authority and they seem to find it difficult to take the position of standing on their rights under international agreements and thus to refuse to give information other than that which identifies themselves."[16] Sometime, though, prisoners were sullen and silent, and Zimmerman resorted to yelling threats to find out what they knew.[17] As the rush of battle possibly turned into the tediousness of interrogations that night of April 1, Private Zimmerman may not have realized that Easter had ended.

April 2, 1945, at the hour when everything was cloaked not in darkness but in a shadowy gray and the chill of morning invigorated while holding the faint promise of warmth, the men of *L Company* began to move about. Folding blankets, grabbing

K-rations, gathering packs and weapons, they prepared for another day of difficult fighting.[18]

As the sun slowly broke over the horizon, the men of the *3rd Battalion* mounted trucks, tanks or any available vehicle. Their destination: Bad Wimpfen. Along the way, they passed places called Hoffenheim, Sinsheim, Adersbach and Hasselbach—for these men, they were meaningless German names of meaningless German towns.[19] The soldiers fought there and quickly forgot the names as soon as they moved on to the next village.

The battalion had ridden in columns a short way when German fighter planes suddenly appeared around Zuzenhausen. Men jumped from the vehicles and ran for the ditches as the planes' guns strafed the road. After the planes had left, the *3rd Battalion* continued on foot. Engineers led the way to clear the area of land mines (sometimes using German prisoners to guide them through), and the rifle companies followed to secure the towns. As they approached Sinsheim and Hoffenheim, mortar and artillery shells fell all around. Because the bridges had been destroyed, tanks could not enter to clear the town quickly. The men worked throughout the day to clear the village, moving from house to house, ducking and running across open streets, shooting the *rat-tat-tat-tat* of machine guns and the short *pop* of rifles.[20] Through the afternoon, Zimmerman and fellow GIs persevered, their weariness replaced by the adrenaline of battle.

Relieved late in the day at Sinsheim by men from the 100th Infantry Division, the *3rd Battalion* once more mounted trucks and tanks and now continued a steady, unopposed advance.[21] Headquarters lost all communication with the battalion because of the artillery fire and the battalion's movement.[22] Concerned that the battalion might have encountered a serious problem with the enemy, Colonel Hatcher agreed that two officers should travel by jeep to find the unit. Hatcher records, "Those two officers, and their driver drove by jeep through the night, but when they reached the last reported location of the *3rd Battalion* [italics added] it was not there. They [the officers] then continued along the assigned route of advance of the battalion and succeeded in overtaking it just at daybreak the following morning… The prisoners captured [by the *3rd Battalion*] during the night were taken by surprise in the villages through which the *3rd Battalion* [italics added] moved. Evidently they had not expected to be disturbed during the night."[23] No lights were used in the pitch dark in order to avoid enemy fire. For the entire sleepless night, Zimmerman and *Company L* had bounced or stumbled along in a painfully slow procession of tanks, trucks and men. Their hours-long journey had advanced them about twenty miles to Bad Rappenau.[24]

In the area, the men of the *255th Regiment* observed the devastating effects the U.S. Army Air Force could have. Anderson remembered, "Over an area covering at least a ¼ mile [*sic*] there were dead horses, dead soldiers and burned out wagons, trucks, halftracks and artillery pieces. It was certain that only a few, if any, had escaped the bombing and strafing. It was truly a shocking experience to see the destruction."[25] The scene of twisted metal and mangled bodies was gruesome.

The *3rd Battalion* enjoyed a blessed day of occupation on April 3. Throughout the cool, cloudy day, a few patrols scouted the area and captured seven prisoners.[26] Replacements joined the companies, units reorganized and, most importantly, men rested and enjoyed a hot supper. As night came, several unlucky infantrymen drew guard duty while the others caught some long-overdue sleep.[27]

The weather on April 4 cleared, but it was still chilly. Wearing their field jackets to ward off the coolness of early spring, the men on *Love Company* crossed the Neckar River and arrived at Waidachshof by late-afternoon to hold the position of reserve battalion with I and K Companies.[28] The *255th Regiment* planned to attack the enemy throughout its zone the next couple days.[29] Rumors circulated in the ranks that a large concentration of Germans was organizing a last stand across the Jagst River.[30] Reserve battalion or not, the adrenaline from all the preparation for attack must have spread.

Move and wait; wait and move. Commanders arranged armies, regiments, battalions and companies around the German countryside like giant chess pieces. On April 5 at 8:11 p.m., the *3rd Battalion* began another march.[31] The day had been rainy since breakfast, and the men were wet and muddy, but they dutifully made the four-hour midnight move to their location along the Jagst River near Neudenau.[32] Double guards were posted that night as heavy mortar fire exploded nearby in Company K's location, and the sporadic pop of sniper rifles around *Love* sounded through the darkness.[33]

Late that morning, the 253rd Regiment led the attack across the Jagst River. The *255th Regiment's 3rd Battalion* supported the attack by feinting action against Neudenau and Mockmuhl and guarding the right flank as the regiments moved slowly forward.[34] Of that day, Anderson of B Company recalled, "We moved from tree to tree, firing as we went. Once in a while I could hear bullets snapping as they went through the trees over my head."[35] The officers of the *255th Regiment* watched the regiment's progress from Countess von Zeppelin's castle at Aschhausen.[36]

It could have been this day when Private Zimmerman carefully led his platoon down the road. The men held their rifles ready; their eyes cautiously scanned the surrounding area. His sister Johanna related that suddenly the guy behind Joe yelled, "Look out!" at the same time bringing up his rifle. With a quick *pop* of the gun, he shot a sniper out of a tree, saving Joe's life.[37]

All during the dreary afternoon of April 6, the *3rd Battalion* fought through heavy resistance in towns along the Jagst River as they assisted the 253rd Regiment's advance of four kilometers.[38] All through the day, they endured strafing from German Messerschmidts.[39] By midnight, *L Company* reached Bittlebronn. The only casualties reported were one sprained ankle and one minor wound in action.[40]

At 3:00 a.m. on April 7, the men of *Company L* trudged out of Bittlebronn and fought their way into Widdern in order to cross the Jagst River.[41] As thick darkness settled, the *3rd Battalion* began to ford the river. Heavy machine gun fire had ignited several houses, the bright flames illuminating the troops in the black water.[42]

All through the night under enemy sniper fire, men of the *255th* walked through the water and scrambled up the muddy bank on the other side.[43] In relating his experience in crossing the Jagst River, Anderson wrote, "[It was] necessary for us to go hand over hand with the water up to our necks. Have you ever jumped into ice-cold water and lost your breath? Then you know how I was feeling at that moment."[44] By 6:55 the next morning, *Company L*, the last of the *3rd Battalion* to cross, reached the other side of the river and joined the advance against the enemy. At 8:10 a.m., I Company faced and repulsed an attack of one hundred Germans thus beginning a day of heavy fighting for the battalion.[45]

Throughout April 8, the *3rd Battalion* attached to the 253rd Regiment to fight the 17th SS Panzer Division in the Hardihauser Wald (forest). In the attack, battalion commanding officer Lieutenant Colonel Schiffman was wounded and taken to the aid station. In visiting him, Colonel Hatcher looked around. "I arrived at the aid station just ahead of him [Schiffman] and it was not at all pleasant to observe some of the more seriously wounded that were being brought in from the Hardihauser Wald."[46] The men had to be vigilant at all times as enemy road blocks, patrols and resistance were everywhere. At one point, two Germans infiltrated the battalion lines and forced two litter bearers to turn back toward Widdern. Despite the fierce opposition, the 253rd Regiment and the *255th Regiment's 3rd Battalion* moved deep into the woods.[47]

Everyone was jumpy that night, always looking for Germans. Strong defensive positions were established, and commanders organized patrols, closely monitored communication posts, and ordered that fifty percent of the men stay awake at all times.[48] Once again, there would be precious little sleep for the exhausted men.

CHAPTER EIGHT

"The rifleman fights without promise of either reward or relief.
Behind every river there's another hill—and
behind that hill, another river."

General Omar Bradley[1]

"I have been extremely pleased with the performance of the 255th
Infantry... When the going gets tough you win by outlasting your en-
emy. You win by having the mental stamina to continue the fight in
spite of any and all things. These take guts—physical stamina and
mental stamina, and the will to win... Your men have a just right to
the pride which they must feel in having the guts and the mental and
physical drive that they have shown the world!"

Louis E. Hibbs, Major General of the 63rd Division[2]

Throughout the clear spring day of April 9, *Company L* and
the 253rd Regiment continued to clear a path to the Kocher

River. By evening, they reached their objective east of Lampold-hausen, and *Love Company* dug in on the wooded hills near the Buchhof farm several miles away from their battalion. Looking across the rolling farmland, they could see the river meandering toward the south.[3] One man in the company had died during the day's action; six more replacements had joined.[4] To an army, these were mere numbers on a page, but for the men of *Company L* these numbers were real people. As the battle-hardened soldiers sat visiting over the hot meal that evening, someone might have quietly mourned the loss of a friend or a foxhole buddy while other men nervously tried to learn about their new comrades.[5] As the day turned to night, the conversations ended, and the soldiers crawled into their carefully dug foxholes for a few hours of fitful sleep and careful watch. "The Germans," according to Hatcher, "were quite aggressive and constantly active in patrol-ling" that night.[6]

The following days began to run together for the men of the *3rd Battalion*. Towns had long since started looking alike; duties and orders remained the same; days and nights ran together; and the sleep-deprived foot soldiers grabbed a few moments rest at any possible time. April 11: "The *3rd Battalion* [italics added] moved…to cross the Kocher River at Weissbach…The battalion advanced against determined resistance receiving heavy sniper fire as well as artillery fire from the enemy."[7] Colonel Hatcher expounded on the fight to cross the Kocher, "The underbrush was burning fiercely on the slope of the hillside across the river but men of the 2nd Battalion were advancing resolutely upward through the burning woods and forcing the Germans farther up the slope. Supporting units of the battalion were wading the waist-deep stream under constant mortar and artillery fire."[8] An-derson wrote, "The 2nd and *3rd Battalions* [italic added] went on the offensive in order to straighten the front line. It was a very difficult maneuver with heavy losses."[9] That day the *3rd Battalion* suffered five men killed and eight men wounded in action.[10] Anderson did remember supplies reaching the GIs on the front lines, and that night they enjoyed the simple yet important pleasures of toothpaste, Coca Cola and cigarettes.[11]

April 12: "*Company L* [italics added]...was alerted to move to Neufels...to hold the town, a key point on the supply line of the 10th Armored Division." *Love Company*, supported the 10th Armored, completed their assignment by 8:26 a.m. Overall, the day was successful and no casualties were reported throughout the regiment.[12]

April 13: According to Anderson of Company B, "The weather on the 13th was beautiful. It was cool and clear." That morning, "B Co joined *L Co* [italics added], riding on tanks and in trucks. We became Task Force La Morte." For the mission, reported Anderson, "We moved to a large curve in the Kocher River, which had been by-passed the day before. We attacked the area and with the aid of the tanks swept through and made quick work of the operation." Later, he noted, "My squad was now only eight men and we found that *L Co* [italics added] was very short-handed also."[13] Even with the depleted force, both companies managed to capture around forty German prisoners.[14]

By this time, the Allied forces were taking hundreds and even thousands of prisoners a day. For the *255th Regiment*, daily numbers of prisoners varied widely—some days the totals were 6, 16 or 21 while other days the total figures reached 40, 67 or 124.[15] Immediately, the captors took the German prisoner's steel helmet since it was often used as a blunt weapon, then they searched for knives, guns, grenades and—sardines of which the German army was well supplied and for which the Allied soldiers had a taste.[16] The GIs then escorted the POWs back to a stockade near headquarters for interrogation. They wanted any information—the strength of the German Army, the location of units, the plans of attack—anything that would give a shred of information to the Allies.

Some prisoners, typically the SS troops and Hitler youth, were fanatical and sullen, and they gave little or no information. Other prisoners were meek and submissive. In a different place at a different time, this German could have been a brother, a cousin or a friend back home, for many of these Americans themselves were sons of German immigrants. However, all prisoners had to be treated as prisoners. News spread of a situation in the *255th Regiment's* 1st Battalion when a "number of the enemy came out to the front of Company A with their hands as though to surrender. When some elements of Company A went forward to accept the surrender, the enemy began a counter-attack. This action was repulsed, and the two enemy who entered Company A's lines were quickly taken care of."[17] Private Zimmerman interacted quite a bit with prisoners as an interpreter during interrogations, and he also experienced a more dangerous side of the prisoners of war. As the family story went, while he was on guard duty one night, some prisoners broke out. In their escape, one German soldier hit Zimmerman on the head with a rifle butt. These soldiers were most definitely still the enemy.

As the men advanced across Germany, they also experienced contact with the civilian population. In some towns, the people hid in basements and cellars while German and American soldiers fought through the streets and houses above. Another village was devoid of German troops by the time the Allies entered, and a priest cautiously approached the American soldiers to request their mercy on the civilians.[18]

Civilians in various villages reacted in different ways. Sometimes they fled before the Americans reached them. In many instances, they stayed, and either quietly watched the tanks and trucks roll through or boisterously celebrated the approach of the Allies. Paul Winkler of *L Company* remembered moving through the towns crowded with Germans who welcomed them with open arms and vodka or schnapps. He recalled two "dead-drunk" troops who had to be helped back onto the truck after "accepting" the greetings. Whether joyful or sullen, white sheets or cloths usually fluttered from the windows. The German townspeople may *not* have been genuinely joyful about losing the war and seeing the American troops, but they knew they could not fight the inevitable.

———

April 14: "*Company L* [italics added]…just outside and to the northwest of Belzhag, holding high ground and a road net… The battalion instituted active patrolling during the period."[19] Sometime during that warm, spring day, Private Zimmerman sat down to write home.

Somewhere in Germany
April 14, 1945

Dear Parents, Sisters and Brothers

As I have some spare time I will drop you a few words. I wanted to write yesterday, but I put it off. How is everybody still getting along at home? Ever so fine, I hope. I am just fine, and couldn't be better. We are getting 3 good meals a day, and the work isn't bad. I hope that I can stay with this, because it sure beats the front lines. I don't care to go up anymore, and I don't think anyone else likes it either.

How is the weather back home, have you had any rain lately? It don't hardly seem possible that April is half over with. In a way it seems like time drags by, and then again it doesn't. I know one thing, the day won't come too soon when we'll all go home again.

I suppose this letter will be about the same as a lot of others I've written, let you know how it is, a lot things we don't get to write about, and I don't know of much to write anyway. I'd write more often if I knew of more to write, the main thing is to let you know that everything is O.K.

I still haven't received any of the Advocates yet, I just wonder what the trouble is. I'd like so much to get it, as it has all the home news in it.

I suppose you'll ask me what part of Germany I'm in, well I couldn't tell you that. I've been to Hidelburg [sic], and a lot of other places that I couldn't remember if I wanted to. The country is very hilly, but beautiful, especially now, with spring here. I wouldn't want to farm over here. I'll take the good old States anyday. I hope that when this is over with nobody will have to come over here again.

How is Grandma getting along, is she still in bed? I suppose she still wants to travel as much as she used to. I think if I'd be that old, I wouldn't want to go that much.

Well, I haven't anymore to say, so will have to close, wishing you all the best in the world, and hope to hear from you again soon.

Your loving Son and Brother

Joe[20]

———————

Anxiously, Joe's parents made their daily trek to the mailbox to look for any news from their son. It was a difficult time—they knew he was on the front lines in Germany, and they knew many boys were not coming home alive. When long stretches of silence passed, they worried and prayed that the son whose blue star hung in their window would someday return to them. Alive.

Finding a letter in that box was cause for thanksgiving and a bit of relief.[21] As she read those thin pieces of paper, Joe's mother cried, saying, "Well, he's still ok; he's still ok. Let's just pray so he makes it back."[22]

For his family's peace of mind, Zimmerman might have exaggerated a bit about the "three good meals a day" and not being placed on the front lines. True, they had been enjoying hot meals in the recent evenings, but chocolate D-bars and K-rations sustained the men during the days and the occasional nights when food could not be brought forward.[23] While these fed the weary soldiers, many might have questioned the term "good." As to his report regarding the front lines, on that day *Love Company* set up defensive positions a couple miles behind the attacking positions. Their time of relative security had not been long, nor would it last.

As he wrote home, Joe surely thought of his mother's home cooking. He might have pictured her standing at the stove fixing pumpkin rolls with potato soup, cheese pockets or fried noodles while his sisters scurried about the kitchen and his Grandma Katherine Heier (who lived with them in three month time periods) helped with the meal by peeling potatoes.[24]

As darkness fell on April 14, the *3rd Battalion* split off from the regiment, and, at Enslingen, once again crossed the Kocher River. By midnight, the men had fought their way to the high ground at Mangoldsall and set up a defensive perimeter, and many of the companies cautiously established a triple guard against the active German patrols that night.[25] Zimmerman's wish to stay away from the front lines had not been granted.

Anderson wrote that the next morning "dawned bright and

clear and we could see for miles." Before moving out, the men hurriedly stuffed a couple chocolate bars and some rations in their pockets or packs for the day ahead.[26] For the next several days, the 1st and 2nd Battalions were assigned to capture the city of Waldenburg while the *3rd Battalion* would clear the towns across the Kocher south and west toward the high ground at Schwabisch Hall. Pressing forward, the soldiers of *Love Company* may not have realized that the commanding officer believed, "The position of the *3rd Battalion* [italics added], isolated as it was by the [Kocher] river from the remainder of the regiment, was constantly a matter of grave concern....The possibility existed that the battalion could be annihilated before reinforcements could reach it in case such a powerful counter-attack should occur."[27]

At 9:00 a.m. all three battalions of the *255th Regiment* began the attacks. Under heavy infantry and artillery fire, the 3rd attacked Westernach with *Company L* entering the town from the south. Army Air Force planes flew overhead calling in observations and adding to the general din of the battles. It was noted in the regimental history, "During the entire day the regiment encountered stiff enemy resistance, sometimes so determined as to be fanatical."[28] By this point, Colonel Hatcher preferred that the artillery companies fire on each town before the infantry entered. While each life lost was considered a tragedy, he believed that deaths so close to the end of the war would be particularly bitter.[29] The battalion lost "only" one man in action that day although twenty-four more were wounded.[30]

As the sun set on April 18, *Company L* approached the village of Weckrieden. The fighting and advance through the area had been constant for the past several days. Their battalion had captured towns; interrogated and escorted prisoners to the rear; conducted regular night patrols; slept in nothing but foxholes; ate little beside K-rations. In his narrative of the battle, Hatcher recorded, "The company [*Love*] was greatly fatigued and not in favorable condition to undertake a fight in the town during darkness," but he presumed the village to be lightly defended. Hatcher therefore gave the order to attack before the enemy could build up additional troops.[31]

Private Zimmerman's muscles ached; his body begged for rest; but he joined his unit that dark spring night as they quietly moved into town. Peering around the corners of houses and barns and darting across a road or clearing, the men of *Company L* quickly spread out. The German soldiers sat in their dark positions—waiting—then with a sudden force, they attacked. For several hours enemies fought with determination, not in a distant, artillery battle but in a close, personal struggle of man against man. Hatcher called it a "bitter" and an "exhausting fight at close quarters."[32] They played a deadly game of hide-and-seek in the dark, the type of game that would haunt the participants for years to come, the type of game where death lurked behind each corner and every hidden sound could be the last one heard.

Around midnight, *Company L* finally overcame the enemy, and the three platoons spread out to occupy the town even though "it was not likely that the troops would be in physical condition to maintain adequate alert and security during the remainder of the night." The adrenaline from battle began to succumb to mind-numbing exhaustion. The cry of "Sleep!" struggled against the anxiety over each sound.

Once situated around the town, one platoon radioed to headquarters of a counter-attack of grounded Luftwaffe (German air force) troops, but they soon reported that it had been "easily broken." Hatcher continued, "A short time later another report came in that still another attack was being made by dismounted luftwaffe [*sic*] elements but that it was not considered a serious threat." A third time, headquarters received a call on the radio of a Luftwaffe counter-attack. However, Hatcher later learned "at the same time a force equivalent to a battalion composed of specially selected and trained assault troops had attacked from the flank." *Love Company* stood alone that night against a force three times its size.

Hatcher vividly recounted, "Just as I reached the radio, the voice of the forward observer, in a excitedly high pitch, called for a second round [of artillery] four-hundred and fifty yards short of the first round. Then, without sensing either round, his voice again screamed over the radio in somewhat unintelligible words…'Throw that…thing out of here! I am getting out of here! They are overrunning our positions!' That was the last we heard from him."

In the silence, Colonel Hatcher had to choose whether to hold back the requested artillery in fear of firing on his own men or to order a barrage a mere four hundred fifty yards in front of the company in hopes of hitting the heavy German attack. He made his decision. "Immediately our artillery began firing at their maximum rate." The colonel learned from liaison officers on a nearby hill, "that very heavy small arms fire and many tracers could be observed about the village. All reports indicated that the fight was extremely hot and that the issue was in doubt…The artillery fire continued."

Love Company eventually grasped the victory. Hatcher noted, "This sort of an attack striking an exhausted company had been almost too much for them. Here again the fighting spirit of American troops, together with the splendid artillery support we were able to bring to bear had turned the situation which had appeared as odds on favorable to the Kraut into a satisfactory defensible situation. The Germans withdrew to lick their wounds and the company continued to hold all of its defensive positions."[33]

Between April 15 and April 18—four days—*Love* lost thirty

men. In a full-strength company of 120 men, that would mean, 25% of the unit had been wounded (20 men), killed (1 man) or reported missing (9 men). Of course, these companies had not been full-strength since they arrived in Europe, making that percentage even higher. Though the company received reinforcements and members continuously returned from the medical battalion, their numbers continued to dwindle.

And yet, the sun still rose the next day. Sergeant Chris Makas heard roosters crowing from nearby farms. Life continued. Anderson wrote, "Spring was approaching. The river flowing eastward into the Danube and the hills turning green again reminded some of us of HOME."[34] No doubt Private Zimmerman had similar thoughts.

———————

While the *3rd Battalion* fought villages northeast of Schwabisch Hall, across the river, the 1st and 2nd Battalions began to attack the castle and town of Waldenburg. Located about ten miles south of the Kocher River, Waldenburg dominated the area from its high seat on a hill seventeen hundred feet high. To be able to move throughout the region and gain control of Schwabisch Hall, the *255th Regiment* had to subdue this stronghold. The Germans, situated high behind the castle walls, held the advantage over the Americans. Again, the determination and strong fighting spirit gained the boys of the 1st and 2nd Battalions the victory. Hatcher confidently wrote, "With the heights taken, the last German organized defensive position of sufficient strength to challenge the firepower of the entire regiment fell into our hands. We still were to encounter small defensive positions but the last battle on a regimental, or larger, scale was fought at Waldenburg."[35]

The troops moved with all possible speed through the foothills of the German Alps, sometimes on foot, many times in trucks. The war was almost over. The American generals pushed for it; the GIs longed for it; the Germans, either bitterly or gratefully, resigned themselves to it. As the advance continued, the battalions moved forward in leap-frog fashion, one battalion trucking to the front to clear an area on foot while being bypassed by the other battalions, then mounting trucks to again drive to the front. For the most part, the Germans had retreated from the area but left a precarious and difficult landscape in order to slow the American advance. The *255th's* struggles now consisted of maneuvering around craters in the road, encountering minefields, and advancing through rough and mountainous terrain, all while dealing with mud from the spring rains. After midnight on April 24, the regiment finally reached the plains leading to the Danube River and pushed forward until dawn, quickly overcoming any small resistance the German Army offered. Throughout the 25th, the *255th Regiment* captured a total of twelve hundred prisoners.[36]

After the days and nights of relentless advance, the men of the *255th* enjoyed one night of rest as division reserve at Langenau. They had moved fast and worked hard. They had thus far successfully carried out their duties. Meanwhile, the 253rd and 254th Regiments fought to make a way across the Danube River.[37]

The next morning, the 255th Regiment pressed toward an assembly area at Gunzburg where they were to traverse the river. In his memoirs, Anderson of B Company described the day as only a soldier could.

On the 26th of April it was a clear day with lots of sunshine. The *3rd Battalion* [italics added] boarded tanks and headed directly to the Danube River. The 1st and 2nd Battalions were to follow on tanks and trucks. Our mission was to check the towns and woods along the way. We arrived at the river shortly after dark and B Co was directed to an area of small fields and some woods. The tanks parked and the Infantry dug our slit trenches. C rations were brought out and we started small fires to heat the cans. Some of the cans contained stew, some were hash and some were omelet type eggs. There was a road between our position and the river. All night long trucks used the road to bring up the pontoons and decks for the bridge, that the Engineers were building, to allow us to cross the river. The enemy would occasionally fire some artillery shells to our side. We would hit our trenches and the truck drivers would get under their trucks. During the night some gas trucks arrived to service the tanks. The 254th had previously crossed the river in pontoon boats and were present on the opposite bank so they could protect the engineers as they worked. The Germans could not see what was going on. Their artillery fire was not accurate but still very dangerous. Searchlights were reflecting off the clouds and gave off a glow. This helped to speed up the bridge building. All of the activity around us gave most of us a sleepless night.[38]

The men started to move over the wide river that night, and by 9:15 p.m., the *3rd Battalion* had made it to the other side without notable incident.[39]

The next day, the *255th* moved down an autobahn thickly congested with American tanks, trucks and troops all trying to penetrate deeper into Germany. Thousands of German prisoners of war trudged through the median in the opposite direction.

Along the sides of the highway sat lines of camouflaged jet airplanes, abandoned signs of German ingenuity.

At Ausburg, the regiment turned off the autobahn and formed two columns of advance toward a bridge across the Wertach River east of Siebnach. Hatcher noted, "The map indicated that the road assigned to the *3rd Battalion* [italics added] was hard surfaced and wide, while the 1st Battalion was assigned little more than cattle trails through the woods." In their retreat, however, the thorough German troops had mined the road, felled trees and created such craters to render it impassible. The *3rd* soon joined the 1st on the neglected trail, but this also proved difficult to navigate. Rain fell throughout the day and the churning of truck tires and tank tracks ate up the solid ground, transforming the area into a swamp through which vehicles had to be pulled one by one. All night the men labored through the sucking mud. Officers nervously pushed soldiers while warily watching for an enemy attack. Hatcher continued, saying, "At one point, while the column was halted on the trail, Lieutenant Colonel Smoak asked me if I knew any prayers. When I asked him why the question, he replied that if I knew any, now was the time to say them."[40]

Finally, the regiment broke through the sludge and rushed on toward the bridge. The 1st Battalion reached their destination just ahead of the *3rd* and quickly tore out all demolition wires. Muddy, wet and exhausted after yet another sleep-deprived night, *Love Company* joined their battalion in silencing small pockets of resistance around the river. By dawn on the 28th of April, they reached the area west of the bridge.[41] Nature had been a less deadly foe than the German soldier, but she was still formidable.

Major General Louis Hibbs commended the men of the *63rd Division*.

Your aggressiveness, professional skill and determination to win enabled you to rise above the fatigue caused by long rapid marches and tough combat throughout an area of rough stream-cut terrain in order to smash the retreating enemy...You have played a splendid part in crushing the last organized resistance north of the Bavarian Alps. I am deeply grateful that I have been honored by being the commander of a fighting outfit such as this.[42]

But the *255th Regiment* did not rest after reaching the bridge spanning the Wertach River. Rest would come after the war. They refueled and continued; their most shocking discovery was still to come. Landsberg lay just ahead.

RIGHT: Theodore (Ted) Zimmerman, father of Joseph Zimmerman, during World War I.

BELOW: Ted and Rosalie [Heier] Zimmerman on their wedding day, 1919.
Both courtesy Rowena Thomas

BELOW: Zimmerman children. Back row: Mary, twins Alberta and Albina (being held), Theresa, Kay. Front row: Eddie, Sally, Fabian, Joe, Johanna.
Courtesy Martina Zimmerman

RIGHT: Zimmerman children in the family buggy on their way to school. *Courtesy Martina Zimmerman*

LEFT: Students of Sunshine School, 1930. Joe Zimmerman center of front row. *Courtesy Martina Zimmerman*

ABOVE: Family picture taken before Joe left for Europe. Back row: Eddie, Johanna, Kay, Joe, Mary, Theresa, Fabian. Front row: Sally, Loretta, Dale, Ted, Rosalie, Rowena and twins, Alberta and Albina. *Courtesy Darrell Zimmerman*

RIGHT: Joe Zimmerman
with his parents,
Ted and Rosalie, 1944.
Courtesy Kay Younger

ABOVE: Martina Ziegler,
Joe's "Darling."

RIGHT: Joe and Martina
*Both courtesy
Martina Zimmerman*

I Love You

I love you dear with all my heart,
and I was so sorry from the very start.
I hope to come back to you some day
and this time I hope its' forever to stay.

I'm glad that soon I can call you my wife,
to live with you a happy life.
We'll live on a farm all our own,
a place we can call our love sweet home.

As I sit here tonight I think of you dear
and I wish so much that you could be it here
I would hold you tight, I kiss you again,
I'm sure it would be like the first night we begin.

At night when I go to bed you are in my dreams
you are so close it always seems
I want you to know as I say so long
that darling to me you'll always belong

J. P. Z - march 1st 19

ABOVE: Poem "I Love You" written by Joe to Martina
while he was in France, March 1, 1945.
Courtesy Martina Zimmerman

RIGHT: Private First Class
Joseph T. Zimmerman, 1944.
Courtesy Martina Zimmerman

BELOW: The row of tank obstacles
called "Dragon's Teeth" in front of
the Siegfried Line on the
French/German border.
*Wikimedia Commons Collection,
GNU Free Documentation License*

BELOW: Men of the 254th
Infantry Regiment getting a hot
meal during the winter of 1945
in France.
*63rd Infantry Division
Association Collection,
courtesy David Ritner*

ABOVE: A German pillbox, one of the thousands that comprised the Siegfried Line. *Wikimedia Commons Collection, GNU Free Documentation License*

BELOW: United States Infantrymen advancing through the Siegfried Line, March, 1945. *National Archives and Records Administration*

ABOVE LEFT: Sign at the Siegfried Line reading, "You are now passing through the Siegfried Line courtesy 63d Infantry Division."
63rd Infantry Division Association Collection

ABOVE RIGHT: Joe Zimmerman in France or Germany.
Courtesy Martina Zimmerman

RIGHT: German prisoners of war captured by the 253rd Infantry Regiment crossing the Saar River. February, 1945.
63rd Infantry Division Association Collection, courtesy Helmut Jung

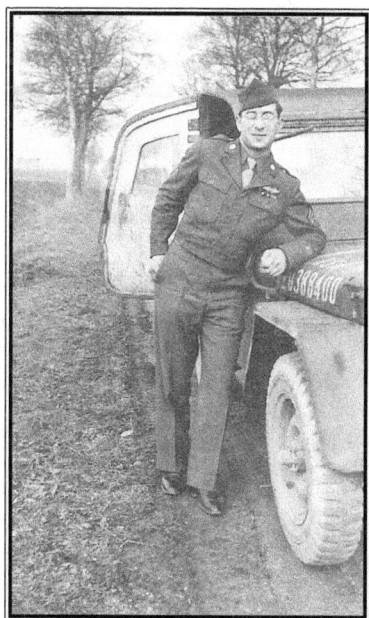

TOP LEFT: A tank-infantry team from the 63rd Infantry Division attacking a German village. A wounded soldier is lying in the foreground. *63rd Infantry Division Association Collection*

TOP RIGHT: Joe (on left) and buddy in France or Germany. *Courtesy Martina Zimmerman*

MIDDLE: Men of the 1st Battalion, 255th Infantry Regiment riding atop an M-26 tank on the Autobahn near Scheppach, Germany in pursuit of the enemy. April 27, 1945. *63rd Infantry Division Association Collection*

LEFT: Joe wrote on the back, "Me and my jeep. A pretty sharp looking soldier, am I not; but I'd make a better civilian, I'll bet." *Courtesy Johanna Dreher*

ABOVE: Soldiers of the 255th Infantry Regiment moving down a street in Waldenburg, Germany, April, 1945. *National Archives and Records Administration*

RIGHT: Members of 63rd Infantry Division interrogate a German prisoner (center). *63rd Infantry Division Association Collection*

LEFT: Members of G Company, 255th Infantry Regiment on the road in Germany, April, 1945. *63rd Infantry Division Association Collection*

RIGHT:
Nazi flag found by Gordon Rintoul in the rubble of a German city. Signed by members of L Company, 255th Infantry Regiment. *Courtesy Naomi Rintoul*

LEFT: Members of the Seventh Army climbing the east bank of the Rhine River. *National Archives and Records Administration*

BELOW: Troops of the 255th Infantry Regiment preparing to cross the Neckar River at Heidelberg, Germany. March, 1945. *63rd Infantry Division Association Collection*

RIGHT: Citizens of Landsberg, Germany, burying prisoners of Kaufering IV concentration camp. *National Archives and Records Administration, College Park United States Holocaust Memorial Museum, courtesy Ilona Shechter, Irving Heymont, Stuart McKeever, Defense Audiovisual Agency, Laurie Heymont Weinberg*

LEFT: Piles of bodies found at the Kaufering concentration camps. *National Archives and Records Administration, College Park United States Holocaust Memorial Museum, courtesy Stephen Adalman*

RIGHT: Bodies of Jewish victims in front of the smoldering ruins at one of the Kaufering concentration camps. *National Archives and Records Administration, College Park United States Holocaust Memorial Museum, courtesy Stuart McKeever*

ABOVE: Portion of a letter written to Martina Ziegler by Joe
while he was in Épernay, France. October 13, 1945.
Courtesy Martina Zimmerman

RIGHT: Joe Zimmerman serving as Mess Sergeant. Standing next to a German prisoner of war (left) who worked under him.
Courtesy Martina Zimmerman

LEFT: Heilbronn, Germany at the end of World War II, 1945.
National Archives and Records Administration, courtesy Harold W. Clover (United States Army)

RIGHT: Sergeant Joe Zimmerman home from the war.
Courtesy Martina Zimmerman

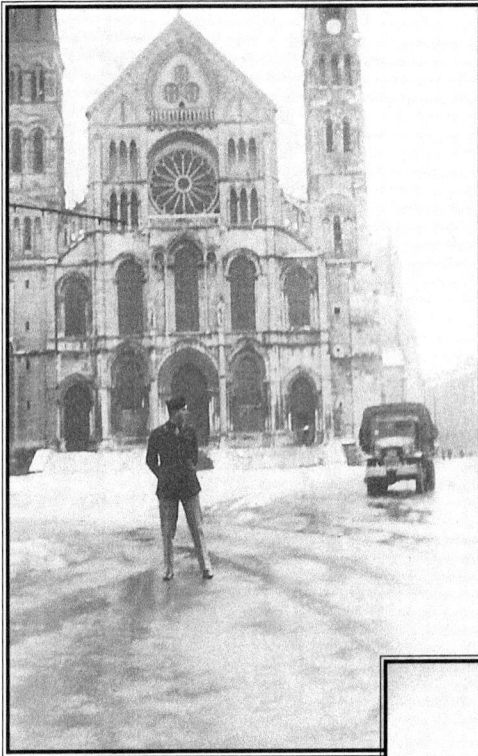

LEFT: Buddy of Joe's standing in front of the Notre-Dame de Reims cathedral in Reims, France. *Courtesy Martina Zimmerman*

RIGHT: Joe Zimmerman on leave. Sitting in front of a memorial dedicated to French tank troops of World War I. Located in Berry-au-Bac, France. *Courtesy Martina Zimmerman*

LEFT:
Joe and Martina
[Ziegler] Zimmerman, 1946.
Courtesy Darrell Zimmerman

RIGHT:
Joe and Martina Zimmerman.
Courtesy Martina Zimmerman

LEFT:
Joe and Martina Zimmerman
with their parents, Ted and
Rosalie Zimmerman and
Adam Ziegler.
Courtesy Johanna Dreher

ABOVE LEFT:
Joe Zimmerman.
Courtesy Martina Zimmerman

ABOVE RIGHT:
Joe Zimmerman with the accordion
he bought in Germany.
Courtesy Martina Zimmerman

LEFT:
Joe Zimmerman.
Courtesy Sally Burgardt

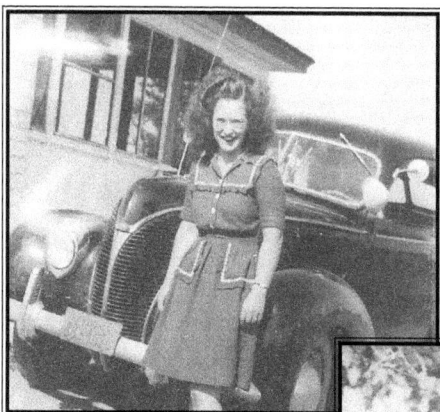

LEFT:
Martina Zimmerman.
Courtesy Martina Zimmerman

BELOW: Joe Zimmerman
cultivating the trees he planted
on his farm. Picture taken as
the result of winning a prize for
his conservation efforts.
Courtesy Martina Zimmerman

ABOVE: Joe and Martina
Zimmerman, September,
1961. One year before
his death.
*Courtesy Martina
Zimmerman*

Joe and Martina Zimmerman's family. Darrell, Jolene
(on father's lap), Joe, Martina, Marilyn (on mother's lap), Don.
Seated in front: Bob, Wayne, Bill.
Courtesy Darrell Zimmerman

CHAPTER NINE

"We all know how precious life is. We spend every day and every hour of the day doing everything we can to stay healthy and stay alive. It is no exception in combat that we spend every minute, yes every second, trying to prolong our life on this earth. And it makes no difference in our faith or our belief, we look to God, or some one for help."

First Lieutenant Jack Kerins, 1st Battalion, 255th Infantry[1]

"The word Holocaust had little meaning to me until my last day of combat in Europe on April 28, 1945."

First Lieutenant Jack Kerins[2]

After refueling in the cool morning, *Love Company* climbed back onto tanks of the 12th Armored Division and pushed forward.[3] Kerins recorded, "It was a beautiful…day and the view of the Alps with its snow-capped peaks was awesome."[4] The 1st

Battalion led the sixty-mile advance with the *3rd* following to search and gather the droves of surrendering enemy soldiers. Occasionally, the Germans offered sporadic gunfire, but, in general, the enemy was on the run.[5]

Early afternoon, the typical day began to change into an experience that would cause many of these battle-hardened GIs to weep. Almost imperceptibly, an indistinguishable odor began to grow. For ten miles the stench became stronger, forcing itself on the soldiers, their minds not able to comprehend the cause of the horrendous stench.[6] Moving with the *255th's* 2nd Battalion, Wes Epstein of the field artillery chronicled his experience. "The acrid smell of death dominated your senses, as a warning that you were about to behold a horror that was beyond description. As a seasoned veteran, no stranger to the sight of slaughter and pain, I was still unprepared for the atrocities I was about to face."[7]

The sky turned gray and intermittent rain showers dampened the men.[8] Through the woods on a small dirt road they walked, hearing and feeling water drip through the trees. While the sun descended in late afternoon, the men suddenly saw a barbed wire fence. Sergeant Vincent Koch of Company M, *3rd Battalion* recounted, "I opened up the doors. The odor coming from there was absolutely unbelievable."[9] The Allied Army first discovered the monstrosities of Nazi concentration camps on April 4, a mere twenty-four days previous.[10] Until that time, they had heard stories and rumors, but no story or rumor could prepare a man for that kind of reality.

Private Joe Zimmerman, like many men, forever kept his heartrending memories inside. Others shared their experiences and thoughts of what they witnessed that day.

"We saw with our own eyes that when somebody couldn't work anymore, through malnutrition, or just literally worked to death, they cremated them, and so we saw stacks of bodies in the crematorium."[11] —John Brown, Commanding Officer of Company K, *3rd Battalion, 255th Regiment*

"The memory of starved, dazed men who dropped their eyes and heads when we looked at them through the chain-link fence, in the same manner that a beaten, mistreated dog would cringe, leaves feelings that cannot be described and will not be forgotten. The impact of seeing those people behind that fence left me saying, only to myself, 'Now I know why I am here.'"[12] —Major Richard Winters, Company E, 101st Airborne Division

"We saw all these people in what we called blue-and-white striped pajamas. It was just unbelievable. The tanks stopped, and we're staring at these people. They looked like they was walking dead. And corpses piled on flatcars. We didn't know what to make of it."[13] —Staff Sergeant Wayne Armstrong, Company C, 1st Battalion, *255th Regiment*

"[The camps were] full of starving and dying political prisoners. These people, many of them recently moved from DACHAU, many of them from the Ghettos of Poland, were found in advanced stages of malnutrition, typhus, diarrhea, skin diseases, boils and abscesses, and mental and emotional illness. The torture and starvation to which they had been subjected were visible on many persons; they walked like puppets—if they could walk; or lay on bare boards too weak to do more than motion feebly to their mouths. Some of them could not speak; others cried like children."[14] —United States Army report on the Kaufering camps at Landsberg

"I noticed a column of DP's [displaced persons]…clinging to each other struggling to walk. It would be impossible to describe their condition. Suddenly one of the DP's bolted from the line and ran over to me, grabbed my hand, kneeled down and began kissing my hand, saying, 'Danke' 'Danke' over and over again."[15] —First Lieutenant Jack Kerins, Company D, 1st Battalion, *255th Infantry*

"An unspoken expression of thanks came from tear filled eyes."[16] —Wes Epstein, 863rd Field Artillery Battalion, Liaison to 2nd Battalion, *255th Infantry*

———————

Just forty miles west of Munich at the foot of the Alps, the quaint village of Landsberg straddled the Lech River through which the frigid, melted snow ran. It was here that a young, idealistic Adolf Hitler was imprisoned in 1924 for several months as negligible punishment for his attempted coup against the German government. Sitting in his comfortable cell, he dictated the autobiography of a crazed human—*Mein Kampf (My Struggle)*.

By 1945, across the peaceful landscape huddled eleven concentration camps named for the nearby Kaufering train depot and distinguished only by a number. In June, 1944, the same month the Allies stormed the beaches of Normandy, the first prisoners, many relocated from Auschwitz, arrived at the Kaufering camps. Colonel Hatcher observed, "The icy breath of the mountains spreads its invigorating blanket over the sun-drenched plains down Landsberg way. What a strange sense of propriety the Nazis must have had to have located the concentration camp for Jews in Landsberg. There the suffering humanity of the concentration camp must have gazed with bitter irony upon the majestic and towering aloofness of the awe inspiring heights of those icy mountains."[17]

The Kaufering concentration camps were work camps. Under the name Project "Ringeltaube," the inmates constructed three underground factories with concrete walls nine to fifteen feet thick that would produce the German jet fighter planes, the Messerschmitt 262.[18] The Nazis transported nearly 29,000 people in cattle cars into the area to labor on the construction. In the eleven months the prisoners toiled at Landsberg, over half of them—14,500—died a slow, cruel death of slavery and starvation.[19] "The finding of the war criminals commission 6823 of the *7th Army* [italics added] notes that the eleven camps in the Kaufering-Landsberg area were the worst ones in Germany in terms of the inhumanity, the hunger, and the illnesses suffered by the prisoners."[20] The factories were never completed.

The captives at Kaufering lived in huts half buried in the ground and so low that a man could not stand straight except in the middle. In each hut measuring 15 foot by 50 foot, 60 people squeezed, eating and sleeping on wooden shelves.[21]

As the Americans approached, the Nazis forced many of the prisoners to evacuate to nearby Dachau. Designated the typhus camp, Kaufering IV held three thousand people who were simply too weak to move, much less walk forty-three miles.[22] So, in a final act of calculated barbarity, the SS guards herded most of the Kaufering IV inmates into their partially subterranean, wooden huts, "nailed shut the doors and windows…hosed down the buildings with gasoline, and set them on fire." The American soldiers saw in the distance "an awful black, acrid smoke" rising.[23] All the women and children died in the gas chambers long before, but half of the men who did not participate in the last minute evacuation were murdered just one day before freedom came.[24] The buildings of Kaufering IV still smoldered as the

255th Regiment arrived.

A high barbed wire fence surrounded an area devoid of all grass, trees or bushes; wretched inmates lay on the bare ground or awkwardly walked about like puppets made of wood and string. Their eyes were sunk deep into the sockets, and bones protruded from their thin skin. Medics carefully moved among the prisoners giving what aid and comfort they could.

Kerins arrived directly in the town of Landsberg, but after hearing of the atrocities, he and his driver went to inspect one of the camps. He recalled how smoke still rose from several smoke stacks in a large factory within the camp. He entered the large building where so many had suffered. One room had been a lab for experimentation. Another room served as a kitchen in which barrels of bread ingredients sat—one barrel was full of flour, the other barrel was filled with sawdust. "The next section of the building contained glowing furnaces, that were hurriedly left unattended when we arrived. From the stench you could tell what the fires were consuming—human flesh. When I left the building there was an 8 to 10 foot deep trench, and when I looked down into it, tears came into my eyes. Many bodies were tossed into the bottom and all you could see was a grotesque array of arms and legs and striped pajamas. I cringed to think how these people suffered before they died." He continued, "As I made my hurried exit, I saw other combat-hardened soldiers with tears in their eyes and vengeance on their faces. Some were nauseated. Some were clutching their weapons and shouting revenge. The memory of that visit, and the lasting sight of many inmates still trying to make their way out of the compound with the help of each other, still haunt me."[25]

The time that *Company L* spent at the camps was short, but the memory of those concentration camps lasted a lifetime. These strong, young men had been through hell on earth. They had seen buddies die a bitter, early death. They had fought face to face and killed their enemy. They had felt terror and prayed in foxholes as artillery screamed overhead. They were the few who had looked at death and lived. Even this could not prepare them for the concentration camps. Several veterans of *Love Company* shared their memories. Bob McClurken recalled the excitement of the liberated inmates.[26] Private Paul Winkler of Zimmerman's *2nd Platoon* spoke about "what you call a hut, so to speak, like one big room that had a dozen or sixteen bunks."[27] Private First Class Terrell Wright, also of the *2nd Platoon*, shared how the Jews struggled toward town to find something to eat before being sent back to the camps for their safety.[28] Private First Class Gordon Rintoul of the same platoon remembers that the "soldiers went in the front [of the camps], and the SS troops went out the back."[29] Regardless of the particular memory, all the men proudly knew one thing: they had helped to liberate innocent victims from the horrors of a living death.

Not sure how to help the suffering prisoners, Rintoul and the other soldiers dug out their chocolate D bars and crackers as a simple gift, though they soon were ordered to stop giving food under the threat of a court martial. The starvation was so severe that the prisoners could not keep the food down.[30]

Soon the commanding officers decided the liberated men should be gathered in one place for safety and to receive medical attention. In an act of kindness that must have resembled cruelty, the soldiers returned the pitiful creatures to the camps. Rintoul shared that they made the captured SS guards clean the camp before returning the freed prisoners.[31]

In the days to follow, the army commanders ordered the civilians of Landsberg to walk through the Kaufering camps since they continued to deny knowledge of the brutality that had occurred.[32] As punishment for their claimed ignorance, the Allies forced the men to carry hundreds of slaughtered inmates to a final resting place in a mass grave.

Records do not show exactly which of the eleven Kaufering camps *L Company* saw. Regiments and battalions, companies and platoons, even whole divisions were spread throughout the area and given orders to travel unmarked roads or simple paths. Some units were the first to come across a particular camp; other units arrived a short time later. Men telling their story simply recall that they helped liberate "*the* Landsberg concentration camp."

It is not important exactly who reached the camps first. Of true value is that every man there risked his life to liberate fellow human beings. Today, the only evidences of the eleven Kaufering concentration camps around Landsberg are these men's memories and a memorial with a few remaining barracks at Kaufering VII. In 2000, the United States Army Center of Military History officially recognized the 63rd Division as liberators, and the division flag proudly hangs in the Holocaust Memorial Museum in Washington, D.C.

The rainy night of April 28, the men of *Company L* dug their foxholes in the forest at Hurlach. They had just been informed that they completed their last combat assignment.[33] Relief from the news was mixed with horror from the day as the men sat through the soggy night; the stench of the nearby camps still permeated the air. Anderson remembered of the next morning, "We were a HAPPY bunch on the morning of the 29th. We had survived, even though at times it hadn't seemed possible."[34]

The 36th Division relieved the *63rd Division* and hurriedly continued an advance toward the Eagle's Nest, Hitler's one remaining stronghold. For the soldiers of the *63rd*, the battles were done. From February 6 to April 28, 1945, the division had spent 119 consecutive days in combat and suffered 8,019 casualties, a 57% turnover rate.[35] Fighting the war was over for the survivors of *Love Company*; now they would just have to fight their memories.

CHAPTER TEN

"The battles are fought; the war is history; but the accomplishments of our soldiers shall affect the lives of men until the sun shall cast its shadow."

Colonel James E. Hatcher[1]

"I wouldn't trade the experience for a million dollars—but I wouldn't give a nickel to do it all over again."

Robert Stuart, *Seventh Army* veteran of World War II[2]

In the darkness of the predawn hours on April 29, *Company L* welcomed a hot breakfast before wearily loading onto crowded trucks.[3] Throughout the day, the men took turns standing and sitting on the floor as the convoy crept along at twenty miles per hour.[4] Each soldier tried to keep his balance in the swaying, bouncing truck for the thirteen-hour journey while he passed the time talking with buddies, eating his K-ration dinner, smoking a cigarette or staring across the passing countryside.[5]

The company stopped in Oberroth, and gratefully searched for houses instead of foxholes for the night. Anderson wrote of entering a house and discovering an old couple sitting in the corner along with their cow and chickens, not an unusual sight in Germany where barns were directly attached to the home. That evening, Zimmerman may have visited with a German farmer, butcher or shopkeeper—people so much like his family—or he may have immediately fallen into an exhausted sleep.[6]

As the GIs continued through Germany's heartland, the rural scene could have led Private Zimmerman's thoughts back home. On the farm, his family worked hard to make a living, but they always had plenty to eat. Their table was laden with what they had grown or raised—from their garden came fresh or canned fruits and vegetables, from their barn came beef, pork, poultry… and rabbits.

As teenagers, Joe and his brother Fabian decided to buy two doe rabbits for one reason or another. Soon they realized they had actually obtained one male and one female, and in the short span of four years, their two turned into three hundred. The family was supplied with more meals of rabbit than they probably cared to eat. One night, two dogs dug under the fence and killed all but a few, thus ending the brothers' business venture.[7] The family might not have been all that sad.

Company L continued with the rest of the *255th Regiment* throughout April 30, this time under the truck tarps as protection from the intermittent rain and late snow.[8] They reached Heilbronn by 8:00 p.m. Commanders of the *3rd Battalion* searched for a place to sleep that night and decided on a large brewery with each company occupying one floor. Remembering the accommodations, Major Boyd said, "At least we were inside and had plenty of beer."[9] Throughout that day, news spread that Adolf Hitler had committed suicide in a bunker underneath Berlin. Certainly the "plenty of beer" available came just in time for their celebration.

With a prewar population of fifty thousand, Heilbronn suffered great destruction. Hatcher estimated, "It would have been difficult to have found a dozen undamaged houses in the entire city. The streets in the main portion of the city were a mass of rubble. Bricks and masonry covered the streets from side to side and only parts of walls of buildings remained standing. Over all this hung the sickening stench of death that lay beneath the debris."[10] In the ruins, Rintoul found a Nazi flag. He commemorated *2nd Platoon's* service together by having them sign the souvenir and then kept it safe in his empty gas mask case.[11]

Major General Louis Hibbs wrote on May 1, "Blood and Fire, you're getting a break, and a well-earned one, from combat. You've fought across the Saar, through the Siegfried Line and across Germany from the Rhine, through the Odenwald, across the Danube to within sight of the snow-covered Bavarian Alps. Victory is on the horizon."[12]

Victory was indeed on the horizon, and the men of the *255th* knew it. Deciding that a brewery was not the best place for soldiers to stay long-term, the officers assigned housing for the men. Small groups spread throughout the local countryside to live with families in houses and on farms. Cooks delivered food and mail each day to the men, whose only duty was to gather for morning exercises and drills and then to relax. The weather in May was beautiful just as spring should be. The grass turned green. In some places, strawberries were abundant. Anderson described his location, "Out back and down the hill was a river valley where farmers raised their hay. We could watch them cut the grass with scythes and carry it off in a wagon pulled by a cow. The women were doing all the chores, as the men left were very old."[13]

May 8, 1945—VICTORY in Europe came at last! The prayers of Private Zimmerman and millions of GIs like him had finally been answered. The nightmarish dreams of Hitler and millions of Nazis following him had finally been crushed. The *255th Regiment* had been out of combat for a week, and none could have been more grateful for the news. However, while the Allied Army could start preparing for the occupation period of Europe, it was still fighting a war in the Pacific. After V-E Day, an increasing number of men in the *3rd Battalion* were reassigned daily to other units.[14] The soldiers waited and dreaded a call that would send them onto the front lines again, especially since those front lines would be against the Japanese. Training for the Pacific War began.[15]

———————

Bad Mergentheim, Germany
May 30, 1945

Dear Force:

Well, I finally got around to drop you a few lines. I am almost ashamed of myself for not writing sooner.

I have been getting the Advocate quite regular now. It took some time before I received the first issue, but now I get one almost every week. Some of them are quite old, but nevertheless it's always news to me, and any news from home is always appreciated. I always read the news of the men in service first to see how the other fellows are doing in different parts of the world.

How is good old Quinter still doing? Boy, I'd like to be back there again. I think I'll get again before long, this time to stay, I hope. I've come to the conclusion that I've seen enough of this world and am ready to go back on the farm again.

Right now I'm doing O.K. for myself, but before I came back with the division of M.P. I was up in the foxhole with the other fellows. It was tough up there and without God's help I don't think anybody could get thru it alive. I never did get hit, but had some awful close calls, which I have already forgotten.

Well, I have about run out of writing space, so will close.

Keep the Advocate coming, and tell everybody hello for me.

I remain as ever,

Joe[16]

Over the summer, the *63rd Division* reassigned its troops as the *Seventh Army* changed its focus from war to occupation. Private Zimmerman never received the dreaded orders to join the Pacific War, and three months after the fall of Nazi Germany, Paul Tibbits flew the *Enola Gay* to drop the atomic bomb over Hiroshima. Japan surrendered on August 14, 1945, and the world celebrated V-J Day. People young and old, civilian and soldier, man and woman breathed a sigh of relief. World War II was over.

Farmers and housewives, teachers and business owners across Gove County, Kansas, received the weekly *Gove County Advocate* two days later. As they read the articles while in the local cafe or gas station, at the grocery store or in their home, they relished the news.

Japan Surrenders to Allied Terms Tuesday Eve

Today, the entire world is rejoicing—and with due cause to rejoice for the termination of the war with Japan brings to a close a world-wide conflict, that has existed for almost 14 long years. The United States has been at war with the Axis nations only a small portion of the time, since December 8, 1941, the day following the "sneak attack" on Pearl Harbor…"[17]

———————

In post-war Europe, the civilians and American troops worked well together. Zimmerman longed to return home. Yet his current location in France was much better than a foxhole on the front line. Always, he thought of his darling Martina.

Épernay, France
Oct 13, 1945

My Dearest Sweetheart:

It has been better than a week now since I last wrote any letters. Honey I am sorry that I neglected you, and I hope you'll forgive me for it. I wrote you one letter while I was over in Switzerland, but I didn't mail it, because I think it will go faster if I mail it from here. I will get it, and this letter in the mail today. I don't know why I didn't write any letters, but the trouble was we were always going someplace or doing something, there was just to much to see, but even that is no excuse for me. I know you will be patiently waiting for a letter from me all this time. I promise it will never happen again. I know I deserve a good bawling out, and if you give it to me, it will only be that I have it coming. I never have waited this long, and again I say I am sorry from the bottom of my heart.

I went up to get my mail this morning, and I had 14 letters waiting for me, 4 of them were from you darling. I opened your letters first and started reading them. I was so glad to hear from you again. I know I can never do enough for you. If you'll forgive me, I promise this will never happen again. You will get these 2 letters before folks will, because I am writing to my loved one first.

Honey you are still first on my list, and always will be. I still love you, and always will. You can believe me I never had anything to do with the women over there, and that goes for this place here too. I love you darling, and I hope forever to keep.

I got back to Epernay last night at 8:30. I should have been here yesterday morning already, but I'll tell you what happened. We took the train from Basle Switzerland to Strausberg France, and from there we took another train to Chalons, France. At Chalons we took the train that was supposed to stay here at Epernay, but it didn't stay, and went right on through to Paris. I never was so disgusted in all my life. I told myself right then that I was through with furlough over here. I never had been to Paris before, and I didn't have very big intentions of ever going there, but this just happened that I did get there. I didn't see much of the city, because it's just like the rest of France. Last night at 5:30 we took the train out here to Epernay, that was the only train that stopped out here, or I would of come out right after we got to Paris. I didn't sleep a bit the night before so last night I was ready for bed right after I got back, outside of that happening I enjoyed my leave to Switzerland quite well, only I wish you could have been with me. The papers and things I brought back, I am going to send to you that will give you a better idea of my trip up the mountains. I also have a few souvenirs which I am going to send to you.

How are you by now my loved one? Ever so fine I do hope. As for me I feel pretty good today. I had a good nights sleep which was something I needed. I told you in my other letter that I thought I was getting sick or the flu, well I didn't get sick, but I didn't feel good all that day. It's all O.K. now so don't worry honey. Darling you mentioned that you get up mornings and don't feel so good. Honey you're over working yourself. I wish you wouldn't have to do so much, work is allright as long as you don't have to overdo yourself, but I'm worried about you and I will be till I come home to you again. I am over here, and not doing a thing you might say. This is Sat., and I don't go on guard till Monday night.

Honey I don't hardly think that I will be home for Christmas. I could be home by Xmas under one condition. You probly won't think anything of this, but I want your oppinion before I would go ahead and do anything. You see here it is. I could reinlist in the army for 3 more years, get a discharge right away, and go home for a 90 day furlough, after my 90 days are over with I would probly come over here again. I don't think much of the idea myself, because I may get out of the army within a year or so as it is now. Darling write and let me know if you would advise me to do this. If you want me to I'll do it, otherwise I wouldn't. I don't like the army, and I'd hate to think of 3 more years of this life. If I'm not home for Xmas, I may be home shortly after. I'd like so much to be home, and I know how you feel about it too, but Uncle Sam still tells me what to do, and until I get out of the army we won't be able to go ahead with our plans like we want to.

Hon. I will answer your letters one by one that way I hope to answer all of them within a few days. I hope that's O.K. with you sugar.

Well we just got back from town, and I will finish this letter to you. I mailed the other one so you will probly get it before you get *this one. I will try to write real often after this. You deserve the best from me, because you are the only girl I ever loved, and always will. I don't know of anymore to write about for now so will close wishing you all of Gods blessing, and the best of everything till we meet again. By honey, and best of luck.*

Yours forever
With all my love
Joe[18]

As difficult as it was to give up an opportunity to go home for Christmas, Martina and Joe decided it would be best for him to stay for his original service term. As the holidays quickly drew near, Private First Class Zimmerman received a promotion to corporal and an assignment as mail clerk. Once again, the army moved him, this time to Soissons, France.

With so many sisters to write him as well as letters from his parents and Martina, Corporal Zimmerman received quite a bit of mail. Whenever he had the chance, he replied to his loved ones, sometimes putting in three sticks of gum into the letters to his family for his younger siblings.[19]

France
Dec. 14, 1945

Dear Parents, Sisters and Brothers:

I received a letter from you day before yesterday and was never so glad to hear from you again, that was the first letter I had since I've been here at Camp Roosevelt. It is so good to hear from you again. I hope my mail comes through more. I didn't get any of my mail from Epenay [sic], but I hope to get it pretty soon.

I am glad to hear that all of you are in good health at home. As for me I'm still OK and about as can be expected. I do have a cold, but that is only natural I guess.

The weather is still the same over here, rain and mud and more rain. It isn't very cold now, but that may not last long. I wish you could get some of this rain, I know you could use it. It's to bad that the wheat isn't doing so good. I was hoping that you would get a good crop next year, maybe it will do better later on.

Well I got another promotion and am now a Corporal or T/5, whatever you want to call it. It doesn't mean anything to me except more money. They can keep all their stripes and send me home. I don't know when I will get to come home, I know it won't be this year anymore, but by spring of next year, maybe, I sure want to be at home.

We are moving again in a few days, it seems like that is all we get done anymore. I hope we stay at one place pretty soon, because this moving sure gets tiresome. The address will be the same so you don't have to worry about that.

It is only 11 more days till Christmas. It doesn't hardly seem like Christmas here, but time always goes by.

I am still doing the same kind of work, and it's not so bad, now that are used to it. I know it's better than standing guard. I don't think I'll have to stand guard any more, just Privates and Privates First Class stand guard (ha).

Well I must close now, and I wish all of you a very Merry Christmas and a Happy New Year. I wish I could spend it with you this year, but will have to wait another year I guess. Good luck to you all and write as soon as possible.

Your loving son and brother
Joe[20]

February arrived and marked one year that Zimmerman had been in Europe. The year 1946 brought new hope for better times. He attended some dances put on for the soldiers and also bought an accordion. Music had always been important in the Zimmerman family, and Joe especially enjoyed teaching himself to play various instruments. Growing up on the farm, the family had very little extra money and lived in a small house with no running water or electricity, but Ted and Rosalie made sure they had a piano.[21] In the evenings and on Sundays, friends and family regularly gathered to sing and play. When he could not sit at the piano, Joe used a harmonica.[22] Music was an important part of his life.

Throughout the rest of Zimmerman's time overseas, the army granted leaves to the men more liberally, and Joe began to enjoy seeing parts of Europe. He moved to Reims, France, the ancient and historic town where General Eisenhower accepted Germany's unconditional surrender. Here he worked and saw the sights with buddies.

Reims, France
January 14, 1946

Dear Parents, Sisters and Brothers:

I will drop you a few lines this afternoon to let you know that I am still fine, and in good health and hope you are all the same. Intended to write you a letter before this, but it seems like I never get around to it. I haven't had any mail now for a few days so have no letters to answer and this letter may be short.

I'm still in Reims and we are still living in the same hotel. I think we are going to move to a different hotel this week, but I suppose it will be O.K. too. I like the place here because our living quarters are good and our food is also very good. I think this food we are getting is about as good as I've had since entering the army.

The weather over here has changed a little and is turning colder, but outside of that it's not too bad. How is the weather back home? Did you get any rain or snow yet? I sure hope you did.

Dad I forgot all about your birthday, but I think it's better late than never so I wish you a very happy birthday and hope that you have many more. I hope that next year we can all celebrate your birthday together.

How are the kids getting along in school? I suppose busy with their studies.

I still don't know when I'll get to go home by spring or summer anyway. I sure don't want to put in another winter over here.

Well, I don't know of any more to write about. So Long to all and I hope to hear from you soon. I must get to work now as I'm in the office with all the brass and top kicks. It's not bad though, I get along O.K.

Your loving son and brother,
Joe[23]

Zimmerman again earned a promotion. In his new position as mess sergeant, he was responsible for requisitioning supplies and preparing meals for around forty-five officers, enlisted men and prisoners of war. Under his supervision were twenty-one German prisoners who assisted in the work. As a bonus, he lived in a private room at the hotel that the army used.[24] Here he had a bit of solitude in which he could play the accordian, write letters and compose poetry.

"A Peaceful Day"

Peace has come again this day,
And it leaves us, without much to say.
To us it's just one of those things,
But deep in our hearts, peace and joy reigns.

One step more, and on the boat we will be,
To sail over the ocean to the land for me.
God has answered our prayers again,
Just listen! I hear the church bells ring.

A friend and I will go to church today,
To give our thanks, and our prayers to say.
We must not stop our prayers, not now my dear,
Because our prayers the Lord will always hear.

Today is Sunday, and a day of peace,
Where we should be happy, and our minds at ease.
I know what most of the fellows think,
I want to go home, because Europe stinks.

I don't like it either, not a bit do I.
But it doesn't help to weep and sigh.
Just remember one thing, will you please?
Over the whole world there is once more Peace.[25]

CHAPTER ELEVEN

"To you who answered the call of your country and served in its Armed Forces to bring about the total defeat of the enemy, I extend the heartfelt thanks of a grateful Nation. As one of the Nation's finest, you undertook the most severe task one can be called upon to perform. Because you demonstrated the fortitude, resourcefulness and calm judgment necessary to carry out that task, we now look to you for leadership and example in further exalting our country in peace."

President Harry Truman[1]

"Really I just dismissed the war. I didn't want to join VFWs or anything like that. I just wanted to farm."

Lloyd Mills, 63rd *Infantry* Division veteran[2]

"It seemed like forever that Joe was gone."

Loretta Waldman, sister[3]

He could not pack his things quickly enough. Not that he had much—the accordion, a camera, a German officer's Ruger he had picked up, some pictures and souvenirs—just a few things to remind him of the life he had lived for the past year. June had come, and he was going home. HOME! Finally, home to the family he missed; home to the girl he loved; home to start a new life.

May 31, 1946, Joe sent a cablegram to his parents from Paris. In a little over two weeks, he would be back on American soil, the good ol' U.S. of A.[4] After nearly two years, Zimmerman would once again possess the gift of a free life.

Paris was the first stop on Joe's long journey to Quinter, Kansas. Soon he was crossing the English Channel and saw for himself the White Cliffs of Dover.[5] In a few days, he would indeed enjoy "love and laughter and peace ever after" now that the world was free.[6]

Just as he had almost a year and a half before, Zimmerman boarded a crowded victory ship to cross the Atlantic. The land loving farmer-turned-soldier still had not grown accustomed to the constant movement of the water, but this time the thought of home somewhat diminished the sickening feeling. On June 14, just as his parents had many years before, he saw the first sign of America, the Statue of Liberty. She had given so many people hope, but these returning GIs fully knew that Lady Liberty had not come without a cost. They stood there with pride…and sadness. Life would go on, but they would forever be changed by what they had given.

June 20, the last forms were filled out, the last papers signed. Sergeant Joseph Zimmerman was officially discharged from Uncle Sam's Army. He took a bus across the state of Kansas to the western plains he called home. His sister Johanna and her husband, Joe's close friend, Lawrence, met him at the station and took him home, his final destination.[7]

The next week, *The Gove County Advocate* reported,

> Joseph T. Zimmerman arrived home Thursday night from Fort Leavenworth, where he had received his honorable discharge from the Army after spending 22 ½ months in service, eighteen months of which time was spent overseas. Joe tells us that he had a fairly easy time of it after the war was over and that he spent his time of recent months as mess sergeant at Reims, France and the job was almost like a civilian job. During the war he served with the infantry and of course the going was rather tough at times. He is mighty happy to be home with his folks the Theo. [Theodore] Zimmerman family and says he plans on spending his time farming and has no desire whatsoever to again travel by water—in fact Joe says it will suit him just fine if he never has to look at an ocean again and yet he wouldn't take anything for the experiences he has had.[8]

The Zimmerman girls adored Joe and loved having him back. During the evenings when the family gathered to play music, he brought out his accordion, impressing everyone with how he made the instrument sing. Their brother had experienced an exciting foreign life and shared bits of what he had learned. He taught them a few French words and told them of the good times, but he was silent about the war.[9]

Physically, the fighting had been hard on Joe, but with good food and rest, his body would recover. Mentally, however, memories would forever haunt him. Focus on life ahead; don't look back; try to forget. This became the goal for millions of returning veterans. For Zimmerman, life ahead meant Martina and farming and family. His parents warned his brothers, sisters and friends not to talk about what happened over there.[10] Don't ask questions. Don't bring up bad memories.

He laughed and smiled, played his accordion and teased his sisters; he worked on the farm and planned for his future marriage; he was a hero home from the war, but the war also came home with him. The fun-loving boy had turned into a more serious man who sometimes broke down crying; the boy who used to spend night after night hunting rabbits, skunks and raccoons had turned into a gun-shy man who, as his brother Eddie remembered, jumped at loud sounds.[11] One night Joe went to a movie with a group of friends and siblings. Someone in the theater set off a firecracker as a practical joke. Everything came flooding back in that one instant, and Joe panicked. His brother Fabian recalled that it took a while for him to calm down.[12] Wars come and go, but they never leave its warriors the same.

When the pressure of the memories became too great to carry alone, Joe turned to his dad. Ted Zimmerman had served during World War I in a hospital for veterans returning from overseas, and he knew the kind of trauma his son had endured.[13] Joe also turned to Martina, his lifeline who walked with him through the transition of coming home. She may not have understood battlefield horrors like Ted could, but she helped in a way like none other—she loved him and offered him hope for the future. Joe revealed his heart in poetry.

"Civilian Life"

In civilian life again my dear
With you so close and always near
Lets hope we never again must part
To go away and break ones heart

Civilian life isn't what it used to be,
Before the war across the sea
But we still give thanks to God above
For saving our dear America we dearly love

No more G.I. clothes or G.I. grub
No more bunks to make or barracks to scrub.
No more Sgt. to give you orders each day
Or listen to what the CO. has to say.

Good by to you old army life
I'll settle down with my wonderful wife
Good by Pvts, Cpls and Sgts too
With army life I'm forever through

Lets hope that wars now have an end,
And war torn cities stay forever mend.
Lets hope the world will stay in Peace
With no more wars or big shots to please.

Signed J.T.Z[14]

Joseph T. Zimmerman

PART TWO

CHAPTER TWELVE

"He was the most thoughtful, kindest, best, most gentle man."

Linda Simpson, niece[1]

"He was a very loving person. He was more quiet."

Rowena Thomas, sister[2]

"If Joe had two nickels, he would give you one."

Loretta Waldman, sister[3]

October 22, 1946, dawned a warm, sunny fall day with just a little more than its share of wind. Martina slipped into her crisp, white dress and clasped the gold locket, a gift from Joe, around her neck. He nervously waited in his brown pinstripe suit.[4] Bridesmaids, groomsmen, flower girl and Joe's little brother as the adorable ring bearer—everyone was ready for the celebration. Surrounded by friends and family, the two at long last became husband and wife, then the party began. An abundant German feast was held in the church basement followed by a lively dance. Fabian remembered that everyone "had a good time that day."[5] No one wanted to miss out on the fun, even Martina's niece who had to run back and forth between watching her father's grocery store and joining in the party.[6] Everyone was celebrating not only a marriage but also the fact that Joe was home and a part of their lives once more.

Joe adored his new bride. With her, he could truly be himself and share his thoughts, his hopes and his dreams. At every opportunity, he told her of his love.

"My Darling"

Tina darling sweet and kind,
Will you be forever mine.
Tell me dear you're always true,
For I love none else but you.

I love you and you love me,
So it shall forever be.
To you my dear I'll give my all
Be it large or be it small.

At night my dear when the sun has set
And you and I again have met,
Life seems more pleasant, and sweeter too,
Because I am once more with you.

As time goes by, and life along,
You are the one in my love song.
The words are clear the notes are true
As we sing together I love you.

J.T.Z.[7]

The new couple settled down in their first house just a quarter mile from Joe's parents. "The old Fink place" (so called since they rented it from a local farmer, Mr. Fink) was, by all accounts, a tough place to live. It was infested with snakes and rats. It was extremely small. But it was home, their home.

Right away, their family began to grow. Donald (Don) Dean was born in 1947; Darrell Joseph came in 1948; William (Bill) Leroy followed in 1949; and Wayne Eugene joined them in 1951. As each boy was born, one of Joe's sisters stayed for several weeks or months to help around the house. To support his growing family, Joe left every week to work on the railroad, only coming home on the weekends to tend his farm. Throughout the week, Martina not only cared for her children but also kept up with the chores, gardening, milking and tending the animals.

Joe, Fabian and Lawrence Dreher all hopped on a train to lay new track in Hugo, Colorado. The labor was hard, and, in Fabian's opinion, it was not pleasant alongside their Indian co-workers who "chewed tobacco and drank from the same bucket." Eventually, their effort paid off, and the boss called the three men in to give them a promotion—they would replace electrical systems after the rail was already laid.

In 1951, Joe's wartime dream of living on his own land came true when the family moved five miles to the farm that Martina's dad had given them as a wedding present. Though the house was still incredibly small (total size was 32 feet by 32 feet), it was a definite improvement. Atop a hill in the western Kansas plains sat the house surrounded by a barn and various outbuildings, "protected" from the howling winds by one lone tree.[8] With the farm, a young family and work on the railroad, Martina and Joe had plenty of work to do.

Up before daylight, they began the day by milking their eight cows, leaning into the side of each animal and hearing the steady *swish, swish* of milk hitting the pail. The work continued as the sun rose. With his stomach full from breakfast, Joe headed out to farm the 160 acres that he owned plus 614 acres he rented. In 1951, he planted wheat, oats, barley, legumes, milo and corn, and it all needed to be plowed, planted and harvested. Martina tended the house, worked in their garden, cared for their 100 chickens. By evening, after the horse, hogs, chickens, Angus beef cattle, and dairy cows had been fed (and milked for the second time), the young couple was surely ready for rest.[9] Joe's youngest son Bob remembered that at the end of the day, his dad would sometimes sit down with his family gathered around him and play German polkas on his accordion.[10] Whether or not he meant to, Joe was passing on a love of music to his children. Finally, everyone was tucked into bed for a few hours before the work started over again the next day.

Joe had farmed all his life. It was "in his blood," you might say. Since he left school after the eighth grade, he had spent each day working with his dad, learning and doing. He never stopped thinking of ways to improve. He took agricultural training provided through the GI Bill; he practiced an advanced system of crop rotation, plowing and terracing; and he read how to enhance farming techniques. Joe had grown up during the Dust Bowl, and he knew that if the land was to produce, it had to be cultivated carefully.

Soon after moving to their new farm, he ordered trees from the conservation district—lots and lots of trees. He planted elms, mulberries, Russian olives, tamarack, cherry, and cedar trees, as well as various fruit trees. He and his boys spent hours throughout the years hoeing and watering and tending those trees, not a small task in the dry plains of western Kansas. Except for the mulberry and cherry, the fruit trees were not successful, but his hard work and care of the other varieties won him an award from the conservation district. Sixty years later, many of those trees still stand as a testament to his dedication.[11]

Not long after moving to the farm, the four boys were quickly packed up and sent to Grandma and Grandpa Zimmerman's house to await the news of yet another sibling. November 6, 1952, Joe and Tina proudly welcomed Robert (Bob) Francis into their family. Although Joe and Martina's responsibilities increased, their growing family gave them joy and hope for a bright future.

CHAPTER THIRTEEN

"He really was a wonderful brother."

Johanna Dreher, sister[1]

"He was a religious man, very much so. He was a good father."

Rowena Thomas, sister[2]

"He had a wonderful sense of humor and made jokes."

Linda Simpson, niece[3]

In a few years, Joe decided it was time to start teaching his sons more about the farm work. In the Zimmerman family, everyone helped out in some way. The "older" boys had been pulling a wagon full of water buckets to the young trees, weeding the garden and feeding the animals for a while. When they reached the age of five or six, Joe decided that it was time to give them even more responsibility.

He was a good teacher. Darrell reminisced that he would "always tell us boys, 'Watch what I do. If you have questions, ask but always observe.' He could tell we were watching and paying attention to him."[4] The boys had to pay attention because they never knew when their dad would decide that it was past the time of watching and time for doing. He taught Bill how to drive on the road from the creek to the house, giving him instructions on how to correct mistakes.[5]

One day, five-year-old Darrell was with his dad a half-mile north of the house. "He turned the pickup around and said, 'Ok, time for you to learn to drive.' He stepped out and said to go to the house, turn around and pick him up. I could barely see. I grabbed the steering wheel, pushed in the clutch, let it out but put my foot on the gas too hard and spun out. There was dirt everywhere. I went for a ways and got the feel of it and turned around. When I got back, he said with a laugh, 'Not bad, not bad, but save my tires.'"[6] Joe kept his sense of humor, even with his boys, and he was a smart man to know not to ride with them on their first attempt driving.

As the boys learned more about the farm, they would usually be with Joe wherever he went. Whether driving the pickup while their dad threw feed off the back to the cattle or tagging along to an auction or the sale barn, a little shadow followed Joe.

In his love for life, Joe could be slightly more impulsive than his wife who would have to deal with the practicality (or lack thereof) of one of his ideas. Don remembered one instance when he went to the sale barn with his dad. Farmers crowded into the smoky building; cattle bawled and pushed around the small ring; the auctioneer droned in his monotonous tone, interrupted by occasional shouts from the bidders. In the midst of the excitement, "vendors from Colorado would be selling peaches or apples. He would buy bushels of them and bring them home, and mother would really have to work hard to get them canned. She would let him know that she wasn't happy."[7] To Joe lots of delicious, fresh produce had naturally seemed like a good idea, and he might have considered a jar of good fruit that winter worth the price of a little displeasure at home.

Though extra funds were scarce, through hard work, Joe and Martina were always able to provide plenty of food for their five growing boys. According to Don, "Sometimes the only thing on the table that was bought was the sugar."[8] Always careful not to waste money on unnecessary expenses, the family even used homemade jelly on their cold cut sandwiches rather than the store-bought mayonnaise. In the summer they enjoyed fresh corn, watermelon, cantaloupe, muschmelon (honey dew), tomatoes, cucumbers and what Darrell remembers as "oodles of potatoes."[9] The melons and cucumbers grew in a big garden down by the creek where Joe had scattered the seeds by hand, covered them over with the harrow and let the rain water the plants. The rest of the year, the family ate the extra produce Martina had canned. What watermelons the family did not eat during the summer, they buried in the grain bins to be enjoyed in the fall and winter, sometimes clear into January. Milk and cream, eggs, beef, chicken and pork were year-round staples that the family produced. Martina's fabulous cooking stretched their food to its full potential and completely filled each stomach. Jolene fondly recalled, "I couldn't wait for birthdays. Mom would make the best birthday cakes. I got to lick the bowl. It was the highlight of my day."[10]

On Saturdays, Joe drove to town for parts or to sell the family's extra cream, milk and eggs at Martina's brother's creamery.

For these special trips to town, he took one of the boys with him. They loved going to see Uncle Butch (John Ziegler). "Well, hello, Snowball!" he called to each nephew as he limped his way, puffing on a cigar.[11] The boys drank the chocolate soda Uncle Butch gave them and read comic books they bought with the nickel (or sometimes even a dime) from their dad. Recalling those special times, Joe's grown sons smiled like the little boys they once were and said fondly, "Oooooooh, that was good. Chocolate soda and comic books—it didn't get much better than that!"[12] And, "Oh, that was good. That was our treat."[13]

———————

A couple years passed, and the Zimmerman family once more anticipated the arrival of another baby. In February of 1955, they welcomed Marilyn Rose into their family of boys. The next year another daughter, Jolene Marie, arrived. Marilyn and Jolene were Joe's pride and joy. He talked and bragged about them to anyone who would listen. Both remember their daddy bouncing them on his knee.[14] These were his girls.

In addition to being proud, he was also very protective of the little girls, and with five older brothers, he might well have needed to be. Sometimes he got upset with the boys simply for not watching over their sisters carefully. Marilyn tripped over a hose in the yard and cut her eye, and Joe yelled at Bill and Wayne for not watching her better.[15] Whether the boys were at fault or not for teasing their sisters or for accidents, Joe always taught the important lesson—take care of the girls.

Girl or boy, Joe deeply loved his kids, and his kids adored him. When at the Zimmerman house, a cousin observed that they would all come running to greet their dad when he came in. Kids were always all over him.[16] He was a tough man, a strong man, a hard-working man, but he was also a gentle man, a man who loved and was loved by others.

As soon as the summer crops were harvested each year, Joe continued to leave for most of each week to work on the railroad. In his absence, he wanted to ensure things ran well on the farm. A hired man took care of the farming for several years until the boys reached an age, around seven or eight, that they could handle the work. "Every time we would ride on the tractor with him, we would watch—how to turn corners and how to judge. He would tell me not to overlap rows so much because it wasted time," Darrell recalled. He was always teaching the boys something, partly because of necessity and partly because he was such a learner himself. Joe wanted his sons to know how to be self-sufficient and how to do the best job they could.

Plowing northeast of the house one day, Joe turned to Darrell and said, "Well, you're ready. You know what to do. When you get done plowing, bring 'er home." Fear mingled with excitement, but his dad was right; he was ready. Once he reached the end of the field, the little farm kid bounced toward home on top of their 1948 Minneapolis Moline tractor. In his mind though, he was quite possibly perched on top of the world.

Later, Darrell learned to farm with the chisel. "I wasn't heavy enough to push the brakes when turning corners, so I had to bounce on them. Every week Dad would have to adjust the brakes because I was always bouncing." Many hot summer days one could look out across the Zimmerman fields and see black smoke trailing behind the old tractor. Slouched on the seat under an umbrella Joe had attached for shade, sat a tanned Zimmerman boy, chewing sunflower seeds and taking an occasional swig of water from the crock jug wrapped with a gunnysack.

The work was hot, monotonous and tiring. To break up the boredom, one day Darrell continuously jumped off the tractor and darted across the freshly plowed dirt in pursuit of baby rabbits, which he promptly deposited in the implement box. His fun lasted only until his dad came to find out the problem and spotted the half dozen bunnies in the box. He then made Darrell turn the rabbits loose and get back to work.[17]

While the two older boys farmed, Joe often relied on the younger three, Bill, Wayne and Bob, to weed the garden, paint and do various other chores closer to the house. Once, as he fixed the hog pen fence with his dad, Bill smashed his finger with a sledgehammer. Even though his parents took him to the emergency room, the finger never healed properly. Fifty years later, the damaged finger still serves as a reminder of that time long ago.[18]

———

Though the Zimmerman kids worked hard right alongside their parents, they *did* make time for fun. Occasionally on warm Saturday evenings, Joe and Martina loaded the entire family into the car for a trip to the drive-in theater. Under the expansive Kansas night sky, black and white films rolled, entrancing the Zimmerman kids and parents alike. Afterward, they headed over to the Dairy Queen for a special treat.[19]

Joe also enjoyed animals. Even the death of a milk cow became a time of mourning for the whole family, a visiting cousin noted.[20] Joe especially loved horses, and this love he passed down to his kids. He owned a big, spirited Pinto that he loved to ride. One day, the horse spooked and reared up, throwing Joe off. He broke both wrists when he landed and had to walk home since the horse ran off. Wayne remembered that his dad was not happy having both arms in casts.[21] Fabian laughed, "That put a little stop in his gettin' goin'."[22]

His adventurous spirit did not suffer long, however, and one summer day Joe gathered all five boys to go buy their very own horse. The six Zimmerman men crowded into the pickup, the boys chattering and bouncing with excitement. Soon they stopped at the ranch of a "cowboy from way back" and looked around in wonder at the dozens of horses. With his boys crowded around him, Joe examined the herd and pointed out a white horse. "That looks like it would be a good one for the boys." The horse's name was Wayne. "Boy, we were all excited. We rode it and were in high heaven. Poor horse never had a rest," said Darrell with a grin. Between the boys and all their cousins who visited, Wayne the horse was well loved. He came with only one quirk. If the gate was ever left open, he took off for his former home fifteen miles away. Two separate times Joe drove after him, loaded him up and brought him back home.

Never did Joe lose his love for hunting, and at their junk pile, he taught his boys how to shoot a gun and to shoot it well. Perhaps flashbacks of the war a decade past crept into his memory as he peered down the rifle barrel, but like most of the men of his generation, he never mentioned it, especially to his children.

He was always watching for birds or animals. Driving down dusty dirt roads, Joe frequently stopped the pickup, and father and son (whoever was with him at the time) would both grab their shotguns. If the prey happened to be on his side, he took the shot but allowed his son the chance to shoot anything on the other side of the pickup. As Darrell remembered, "a lot of times we weren't ready and would miss, but he never got mad." Not only did Joe constantly and patiently teach his sons; he enjoyed it.

Nighttime offered another opportunity for the men's hunting escapades. Joe continued this childhood tradition and with two sons searched for jackrabbits for the bounty or cottontails for a tasty treat. Slowly they drove through the darkness scanning the area with a spotlight he had mounted on the pickup. If the excursion had been successful, the next day skinned rabbits hung from the rafters of their chicken house in preparation for the next family meal.[23]

Sundays for the Zimmermans were truly a day of rest. All nine people again crowded into the family car and drove to Collyer for mass at St. Michael's Church. Whether he was naturally inclined toward religious worship or he was driven to it through his horrific war experiences, Joe Zimmerman devoutly worshipped God.

The priest's liturgy echoed in the stone cathedral as the family listened. Joe never allowed his children to disrupt mass, and all five boys sat silently in the pew, their heads stair-stepping down from the oldest to the very youngest. After filing out of the church, they visited Adam Ziegler, Martina's dad, before heading home for a simple dinner of hotdogs and mustard.[24]

Sunday afternoons were paradise for the kids. The day was often spent with aunts, uncles and the endless supply of cousins. The boys fished or swam, swinging over the creek on a rope like Tarzan. Or they rode Wayne the horse or played in the barn or challenged each other to games of kick the can, hide and seek, and tag. Or they all gathered in the evenings to sing and play music.

True to his religious devotion, Joe wanted to give back to God part of what God had graciously given him. He wanted at least one of his sons to become a priest. Twelve-year-old Don replied, "Well, Dad, I think I might like to be one." Was his dad ever proud! The next opportunity, he told the sisters at St. Michael's who taught his kids their catechism that Donnie was going to be a priest.[25]

Christmas was another special time for the family. Most years, snow covered the ground once winter set in. The family hauled a Christmas tree into the house and decorated it, and in the evenings Joe played Christmas songs on his accordion.[26] Unfortunately, little Jolene was usually sick and confined to her parent's bedroom throughout much of December, for, unbeknownst to the family, she was allergic to evergreen. So, Jolene often suffered while the family celebrated.[27]

On Christmas Eve, the family gathered to open presents. Many times, the kids received socks, gloves or other practical gifts, but again, Joe and Martina did their best to make the time as special as possible.[28] One year Joe bought a used bicycle, fixed it up, gave it a fresh coat of paint and presented it to his boys.[29] Another time he bought bride dolls for the girls, one with brown hair for Marilyn and one with blonde hair for Jolene.[30] The kids treasured these gifts their parents sacrificed to give them.

After opening presents, the family bundled up to attended midnight mass in celebration of the birth of God's Son. Joe sang in the choir, his deep voice joining those of neighbors' and family's. Returning home, they walked back through the door of their farmhouse; the smell of the ham Martina had in the oven filled the air and made everyone's stomachs growl, even at that late hour. They sat around the table for the special nighttime Christmas meal of ham and raisin bread and a little wine their dad poured into each glass.[31]

The next day the Zimmermans visited family, eating the feast their German mothers, aunts and grandmother had prepared. In reality, Christmas with extended family was not much different than the frequent Namenstag (Names Day) celebrations. Many times the feast on Namenstag was more elaborate, but whether Names Day or Christmas, the family celebrations were special, boisterous, and always full of fun.[32] The kids played outside in the snow; the adults played Pitch and Pinochle inside; everyone ate, played, chattered and eventually gathered around music. Joe played the accordion, his brother-in-law, Lawrence Dreher, strummed the guitar, and brother Dale often played the piano. Everyone sang.

Musical events extended to barn dances throughout the year. Any chance they could find, neighbors and family gathered in a hayloft, sometimes Ted and Rosalie Zimmerman's, Lawrence and Johanna Dreher's or a neighbor's. Music and laughter burst from the stone and wood structures.

Joe centered his life around family, both immediate and ex- tended. At times though, he and his dad argued. Ted was wiry and tough as nails, determined to win each disagreement. Joe was not much taller but more muscular and possessed a gentle personality. Both men were strong and stubborn. After one par- ticular bout, Joe sadly said, "I just don't know why we can't get along."[33] While they may have had some disputes, often it was his dad to whom Joe consulted for advice.

Though he sometimes stood up to the Zimmerman men, he melted when it came to the women in his life. With Martina, Joe shared his soul. In many ways, they were so different, yet, in many ways they were so much alike. When their kids were around, they often spoke in German to each other.[34]

I took a walk one sunny day
With strided foot steps all the way.
My journey never had an end
So help I ask from you my friend

To walk through life it always takes two,
One by himself will never do.
I think I've got the girl to share
Those wearied steps we all must bear

We will go through life hand in hand
All through the years on American land
God gave the rights to everyone
Of grief and sorrow and sometimes fun
Come on my dear let's have a smile
As we go through life mile after mile.

J.T.Z.[35]

Of course, he continued to strongly protect his daughters. When Jolene was five, Joe took her to the hospital to remove a growth from under her eye. She was terrified of the nurses, shots and entire procedure, and when it was over, she buried her head in her daddy's shoulder.[36]

The other women whom he loved and cared for were his sisters. Decades later, each sister remembered Joe as "real thoughtful, never intentionally hurting us," or they recalled his "good manners" and that "he didn't lose his temper."[37] Coming in from work outside, Joe often helped the girls prepare supper if it was not ready.[38]

"He spoiled Bina and me rotten," said Bert. "He'd loan us his truck when we had a place to go. He was really good to us girls." And when twin sisters Bert and Bina returned his truck with its empty gas tank, their easygoing brother never said anything about it. All he would do was fill it up, always willing to let them use it again the next time.[39] Bina fondly affirmed, "He was like a dad to us, always looked out for us, always a nice, caring man. I couldn't have had a better brother."[40] Wanting someone to play the piano while he played the accordion, Joe sat down with Bina and taught her to play. She recalled years later, "It didn't sound too bad. He taught me what I know on the piano."[41]

In the years after he was married, Joe spent more time with his younger siblings—those who had been like a separate family from the older Zimmerman kids. (In fact, Rene was just three years older than Joe's oldest son, Don.) As they helped on his farm or came for the many family get-togethers, Joe's sisters grew up knowing and loving their brother. Mercifully, they had time to make memories together, for those memories would have to carry them through the years to come.

CHAPTER FOURTEEN

"The doctor said, 'You know your brother won't live.' It was like someone hit me in the stomach. I didn't say anything to anybody. In those days, you or the doctors didn't say, 'You're going to die.'"

Rowena Thomas, sister[1]

"I took my kids and went to see him in the hospital the morning that he left. That was the last time I saw him alive."

Johanna Dreher, sister[2]

Something was wrong. Intense headaches, blurred vision and dizziness started plaguing Joe. He went to the doctor in Quinter to no avail, so he visited doctors at the veteran's hospital in Denver, Colorado. He did not have time to be sick. His youngest was barely a toddler; his farm required attention; he still worked for the railroad; he had a family to support and a wife to care for. But the headaches—the pounding, debilitating headaches—

would not go away.

After the fall harvest was over, Joe's health suddenly and drastically demanded attention. Martina wrote a letter to his employers to explain the situation.

Dear Sirs:

I am dropping you a line to let you know Joe had planned on going back to work the latter part of this month. But sickness kept him from going.

On the 15th day of Oct. just before the noon hour he went into convulsions. We rushed him to the Quinter Hospital. The doctors checked him over. Everything checked out okay. But they wanted to keep him a few days. He told them he was to see his two doctors out at Denver Fri. afternoon for checkups. They released him then Thurs. He took the train that afternoon at Oakley. When he reached Denver he called a cab and they took him up to the hospital. This is where he still is. They have been running tests, taking x-rays and what have you. Still nothing showing up. But he still has his headaches and is weak and seemed somewhat to have lost his sense of balance. He is improving on his sense of balance.

Yesterday a nerve and brain specialist [sic] were to come in and check him. I hope they find out what caused the convulsion and whats causing the other things now.

He doesn't know when he'll be released. If there is to be surgery it'll be a long time and if no surgery he may get to come home by the end of this week.

Our deposit agent "Roberts" called to Salina for Joe and asked for another ninety day leave. They gave it to him. That would put him back to work the latter part of Jan.

I believe that is the answer you want on line #6.

Thanks in regard to reading this letter and I hope you will un-

derstand why he is unable to return back to work. You probably will hear later on from some of the doctors whom are caring for him now. So until then:

I am Sincerely Yours[3]

Once in Denver, Joe faced questions, tests, more questions, probing, still more questions and uncertainty. What was wrong? Why was this happening? When would the headaches and seizures go away? What about his family? Finally, the results came back. Joe had a brain tumor. Doctors scheduled surgery. The entire Zimmerman family was terribly shaken. Bina simply said, the news was "really, really upsetting."[4]

"Dear Kay..." Joe wrote his oldest sister with the revelation. It was a letter she would never forget. Her younger brother, the boy she grew up with, the boy who drove the family buggy to school as they all huddled under heavy blankets, the boy who made their childhood toys, was suffering in Kansas. She suffered for him halfway across the country in California.[5]

Thankfully, insurance through the railroad covered the hospital visits and treatments, providing for Joe what many farmers did not posses. Also, his sisters Mary Racette and Johanna Dreher lived with their families in Denver and graciously provided support and a place for Joe and his family to stay during visits.[6]

Sterile, white hospital rooms, doctors and nurses scurrying around, preparation for surgery, a last look, a final touch...then Joe was wheeled into surgery. Several hours passed before the doctors reported the outcome. The tumor was on the right side of his brain, and it had been pressing on main nerves that affected vision and prompted seizures. Only a part of the tumor could be removed in fear of possible nerve damage that might have caused blindness or inability to speak.[7]

The family questioned and speculated as to what had caused

the tumor. Was it the result of a blow to the head he had received during the war? Or had it started even earlier than that? Was that the reason he needed glasses as a teenager? Was that why he sometimes could not see very well at night and would drive into a ditch? The only answer from the doctors was simply that the tumor had been growing for a long time.[8]

The family believed the surgery to have been mostly successful. Much of the tumor had been removed, and a new treatment called radiation would take care of the rest. Joe could heal and continue through life. The doctors did not mention that Joe did not just have an unexplainable brain tumor—he had cancer. Fabian overheard them discussing the case and asked how much time his brother had. They grimly answered, four years, adding the directive that this fact should not be shared with anyone. It was a day when the term "cancer" was new; it was a day when doctors thought it best to keep death sentences as quiet as possible; it was a day when, instead of being able to share the burden, Martina and Fabian had to bear the knowledge of the truth alone.[9] A short time after surgery, the doctors stopped the radiation treatments.[10]

Everyone soon gathered for the marriage of Loretta Zimmerman to Bob Waldman. Loretta remembered during that happy day, "Joe never complained."[11] Everyone was grateful he had come safely through the surgery, and they were ready for a reason to celebrate. With usual German gusto, they ate, drank, sang and danced their way to what would certainly be a brighter future.

To observers, Joe and Martina calmly carried on the tasks of daily life as well as they could, although he still endured constant headaches. Within, however, they must have withstood terrible heartache. Joe looked at his family and knew the time was short for him to care for them. Worry would not help. Sadness would not finish the work. He had to get busy now.

The original house on their farm was inadequate. The nine Zimmermans squeezed into the one thousand square foot home—just enough space for a kitchen, living room and three tiny bedrooms. There was no bathroom; the family used an outhouse. The boys' room, in fact, was so tiny it tightly held one double bed and a dresser, allowing barely enough space to walk in between them.[12] The four oldest boys slept crossway on one bed.

Eventually, the couple proudly bought a two-story farmhouse six miles away and hired trucks to move it to their farm. What a relief it was the day Joe saw it slowly coming down the road: a house that would be suitable for his family as they grew older and bigger. Once it was anchored on the foundation, Joe and Martina worked hard to plaster the walls, sand and refinish the floors, add a bathroom and pipe in running water.[13] The additional tasks added strain on their already stressful lives. The farm still required attention; the animals needed care; the headaches and cancer continued to loom, but they worked together to complete the job.

The boys had been helping with the work for some time, but Joe realized they would soon be faced with a larger burden. They would no longer be helping but running the farm and caring for the family. The necessity of teaching them became sadly important, for he knew his kids would have to grow up before their time.

They needed a bigger tractor, and Joe had his eye on a diesel at an upcoming auction. Eleven-year-old Darrell went with him. Watch the others when you bid. Wait for the right time. Keep your cool. Stand firm. All these things his father taught. After winning the bid for the "new" WD-6 tractor, Joe turned to his son and said, "You know the way home. Do you want to drive the pickup or the tractor?" "Tractor!" young Darrell proudly replied.[14] The boy was excited to run a faster, bigger machine, but Joe was relieved to have one more thing that could carry his family through many years ahead.

Joe's headaches were both a blessing and a curse to his two little girls. Normally, he worked in the fields or barn, but with the onset of the pain, many days he stayed in the house. To help Martina, he watched the girls while she focused on something else. For Jolene and Marilyn, these were times their dad played with them, times they would not have otherwise been given. But those special moments became fewer as he grew worse. All Joe could do was lay in bed and demand that the kids keep quiet. His illness was confusing to Jolene. "When he got worse, I couldn't understand why he couldn't get up and play with us. I was just so sad he couldn't."[15]

The younger boys' memories of their dad was mostly of his sickness. Around five and six when the doctors discovered Joe's tumor, Bob and Wayne grew up seeing their dad suffer from dizziness and random black outs. He was not able to spend as much time with them as he had with the older boys and the younger girls. Bob recalls trips to Denver to see his dad in the hospital.[16]

Bill, on the other hand, remembered being left at home with Aunt Rene and Aunt Loretta when his parents made the trips to Colorado. He was the son who most closely resembled his dad: quiet and thoughtful, yet strong and independent.[17] Bill enjoyed learning how to farm. He found the work interesting, and he longed to spend more time with his dad, time that simply was not there.[18] "Kind of heartbreaking to have him there and us here. They were bad memories."[19]

As the oldest, Don had the most years with his dad, but he

had made the early choice of becoming a priest. With that decision, he took the great responsibility of the training and separation. After several years of the family suffering from Joe's cancer, the time came for Don to attend high school in Oklahoma City. He was fourteen. Since Joe and Martina could not make the trip, his Uncle Fabian drove him to school.[20] Scared and uncertain of the future, Don left home to become a man when he was yet a boy.

It was a blessing to the struggling family to have relatives who were able to help them. Martina could not be with the husband she dearly loved each time he had a seizure, each stay in the hospital (Denver or Quinter) or during each test that was run. For the sake of her children and the family's income, she stoically continued the work of running the farm in her husband's absence.

Seventeen-year-old Rene, who worked in the Quinter hospital, often checked on her brother Joe during the many occasions he was admitted. When her shift was over each night, she sat at his bedside to visit or to hold his hand until he went to sleep. Several weeks after his surgery, the stitches on Joe's head started to come out instead of dissolving. It caused an infection where his glasses rested, and the doctor told him they needed to be removed. Joe agreed but wanted Rene to be with him. Brother and sister sat together, both trying to be strong for the sake of the other. He was silent throughout the process, but Rene could feel his pain through his nearly bone-crushing grip on her hand.

Eventually, a hospital intern told Rene about a friend of his who had just died from a brain tumor. At that point, all hope that Rene held for a cure ceased. She recalled, "He said, 'You know your brother won't live. They couldn't take the whole tumor in Denver.' It was like someone hit me in the stomach. I didn't say anything to anybody. In those days you and the doctors didn't say, 'you're going to die.' They just did their best. I kept it to myself. I knew I couldn't tell my parents because they were so emotional. It was hard; it was very difficult."

Seeing her brother day after day in such condition and bearing the weight of the knowledge of his impending death became a burden nearly impossible to bear and a risk to her own health. She developed ulcers, and doctors advised that she move to California to live with family. Around the same time that Don left for school, Joe's youngest sister Rene, who had been such a support, also moved away.[21] Life was beyond his control, and it upset him greatly. As he lay in bed helpless and wracked with pain, Joe saw other people able to continue with life. He was being left behind.

Joe and Martina Zimmerman were loved not only by their own family but also by many friends and neighbors. They had grown up in the rural community, and they valued the friendships they had cultivated through the years. The Zimmermans sometimes left their children with a babysitter so they could go dancing or visiting. At other times, they invited people to their home and played cards late into the night.

The quality of these friendships became evident as Joe's disease worsened. Many neighbors were of the Dunkard Brethren faith. As they saw the need, these friends rallied with their tractors to help the Zimmermans work their land. Another time, they labored next to the Knights of Columbus to roof the barn while the women cooked a feast. Though their beliefs differed, the Dunkard and Catholic neighbors respected and valued each other.

"Friendship"

Friends we love, and friends we share
Friends we have everywhere.
All along our friendship goes
Down the painful ways of life's long roads.

My friends are yours, and your friends are mine,
Some friends are good and always kind.
If friendship lasts among our friends
It'll go along till our life ends.

Be kind to friends for they're kind to you.
To me a friend is always true.
I need not tell you what friendship means
To good kind people, friendship always leans

Signed J.T.Z.[22]

Four years passed. Fabian thought his brother might just have exceeded the doctors' expectations and beaten the cancer.[23] Now, instead of dread, they might look forward to a brighter future. As hope began to glimmer, the headaches and seizures attacked with a debilitating force. Throughout the summer of 1962, as sons, brothers and neighbors worked his land, Joe lay in bed at home or in the hospital. It became apparent that another surgery was imperative.

August came and Martina and Joe made the journey west to Denver one last time. After the surgery Fabian thought he "seemed to be doing really good." But the doctors drew him aside and, as they had said five years previously, his brother "would not make it, but not to tell anyone." Joe, on the other hand, felt the surgery was successful.[24] Johanna brought her kids to see their uncle the morning he left the hospital. His face was bruised, but he was positive.[25] They loaded into the car that hot August morning and headed for home.

As they drove, Joe was happy. His mind was full of plans, of all the things he wanted to do. Five years of his life had been taken from him, and now he could finally live. Since his weakened body easily grew tired, they stopped the car by the side of the road at Sharon Springs, Kansas. Joe walked to a spot under a tree where he lay down and closed his eyes to take a nap.[26]

CHAPTER FIFTEEN

*"We didn't even know that it was as serious
as it was until just before he died."*

Alberta Knoll, sister[1]

*"Especially in my teenage years, it bothered me more. Especially
when you're going from being a boy to a young man. Just what's
life all about? Just things you want to ask. For a long time, it just
felt like you were in a fog, just basically existing. [But]
life went on. The farm had to go on."*

Bob Zimmerman, son[2]

Just three weeks after the surgery, a beautiful Indian summer
day dawned. Joe woke up that warm morning feeling better than
he had in ages. He needed to leave the house, to get out, to look
around, to enjoy the day. By George, he wanted to check on the
workers cutting his ensilage. Martina was scared. "You are not

leaving this house!" she insisted. "Yes, I am," he stubbornly retorted. Finally, she agreed as long as he would be careful and not *do* anything but look. With excitement, he slid into the passenger seat in the truck. He and fourteen-year-old Darrell drove around all day, hauling ensilage and checking on the work, talking and dreaming of future plans.

It would be the last good memory Joe would have, for early the next morning on September 18, 1962, he suddenly became worse. The kids rushed to get ready for school, until some of them were called into their parent's bedroom. They quietly stood, their mother nearby, their daddy lying on the bed. In a quiet monotone, the priest administered the last rites as Joe himself pleaded, "I don't want to leave my family. God, I don't want to leave my family."[3] By mid-morning, while the family watched, their daddy, husband and strong provider died.[4] An ambulance rushed up outside, but it was too late.[5] Joseph Zimmerman was just thirty-eight years old. No longer would the kids have to see their father tortured by pain, but no longer would they be able to see their father—the man they ran to greet, the man who made his accordion "sing," the man who deeply loved and cared for his family.

Joe's sister Sally was busily working in the kitchen of the grade school in Park, Kansas, when she looked up and saw her soft-spoken mother coming down the steps. "Joe died of cancer, and we didn't know it," she sobbed.[6] The family was shocked to learn that the "tumor" from which Joe had suffered was indeed the mysterious and deadly disease.

As the saying goes, no parent should have to outlive a child. Ted and Rosalie had endured the tragic but expected loss of two-year-old Emma decades before. But the painful death of their oldest son was heart wrenching. They had prayed for him through two years of the army. They had worried and rejoiced.

They had helped him through the terrible memories. They had swelled with pride as he married and added to their number of grandchildren. They had agonized each time he traveled to Denver for another checkup, another test, another surgery. Now he was gone. All those years were over in an instant, reduced to poignant memories and "what ifs."

Don had just returned to Oklahoma City for his second year of seminary in August. That fateful September day, Father Paul Donovan took him out of class and up to the dorm room. There he told the boy his dad had died. The kindly priest drove Don, numb from the news, the three hundred fifty miles back home.[7]

Family, friends and neighbors quietly and sorrowfully filled the church for Joe's funeral. Sally stated, "Joe had such a big heart."[8] The many people he had touched wanted to pay their last respects. For the kids, from six-year-old Jolene to fifteen-year-old Don, their dad's funeral was a blur, something that they would not or could not remember in detail. Kay remembered her brother as a good student and poet, her brother who would never visit them in California.[9] Sally lost a protective brother to whom she had grown especially close during her divorce.[10] Fabian lost the friend with whom he had hunted and played as boys, farmed and worked next to as men. "It took a lot of life out of me when it [Joe's death] happened."[11] Linda recalled her Uncle Joe as always working but also taking time to give tractor rides when she visited the farm.[12]

The Knights of Columbus and Dunkard Brethren continued to help the Zimmerman family with the farm throughout that fall, but eventually, Martina and the kids had to adjust to life on their own. The farm was their income, and they had to keep it running. Marilyn spoke for them all when she said, "The family stuck together and made a go of it. [We] kept the farm going and just did it."[13] No, it was not easy or fun, but they did it. Fabian helped his brother's family with the farm when he could. But Joe had taught his sons well, and Fabian remembered, "Darrell and Don already knew what to do. I'd just get them started."[14] It would be Darrell and Don who would teach the younger boys to drive and farm.[15]

Don had to choose between returning to school in Oklahoma or staying home with the family. For a sophomore in high school, such a life-altering decision was difficult. He not only wanted to fulfill his father's wish that he become a priest, but he also did not want to abandon his family. His mother kindly told him, "Donnie, whatever you want to do, that's ok."[16]

Martina never forgot her one and only love. As a strong German woman, she continued with life because she needed to, because she had seven children, and because she expected no less of herself. But deep inside, she would always miss Joe. The days slowly became months; the months moved into years; the years swiftly turned into decades. As time passed, she watched as her family grew, children married and grandchildren and great grandchildren were born. She cherished the family she and Joe had. He would have been proud.

EPILOGUE

"I don't even know what it's like to have a dad."
Bob Zimmerman in conversation with a rebellious friend[1]

"Sometimes I just wonder what it would have been like."
Child of Joe Zimmerman in conversation with Johanna Dreher[2]

"I don't have a daddy anymore."
Jolene Zimmerman overheard by Rowena Thomas[3]

"I missed having a dad."
Bill Zimmerman[4]

Sometimes it is difficult to see greatness in people, for normalcy of daily life tends to overshadow the big picture. What is special about a midwestern boy growing up in the 1930s? Why is one soldier amongst millions considered extraordinary during the 1940s? Does one farmer who toils day and night to provide for his family really matter? Why would a husband, father, son or brother stand out as someone unique when the world is filled with these average men? How can one person who has never made the headlines, never led a country or starred in a movie, had little schooling and left no great discoveries be particularly memorable? Why is Joseph T. Zimmerman to be remembered as a remarkable man? Why?

Because he selflessly touched people's lives.

Such a life poured out for others is nothing less than great. A legacy appears as one looks at the rewards of a life well lived—results that may only emerge decades later.

The boy of the Dust Bowl became the man who helped pioneer conservation, quietly alerting future generations of the dangers of stripping nutrients from the land. He was important not because of a great agricultural feat but because he was one man who willingly learned and then taught a better method.

The soldier of World War II became a liberator to fellow human beings whose only crime was that of living. He was important not because he held the power of a general but because he shared the freedom of an American.

The son, the brother, the uncle became the source of joy to father and mother, to brothers and sisters, to nieces and nephews. His smile, his laughter, his music, his helping hand made him special to each person. He was important not because he chose to look upon them but because he cared to see them.

The husband became the lover and provider to Martina. He was important not because of the decades he spent with her but because of the selfless devotion he poured out to her.

The father became a hero to sons and daughters. He gave his time and his knowledge, his values and his love. He was important not because of vast material possessions he owned but because of the large portion of himself he gave.

Such a life, no matter how average it may seem, leaves a nearly blinding impact on those who look past the shadow in order to see the man. Some people may ask God, what if Joe Zimmerman had not died so young? I wonder, what if he had not lived so well?

APPENDIX A

Infantry Assignment of Joseph T. Zimmerman
February 13, 1945 – Summer, 1945

**Supreme Headquarters Allied
Expeditionary Force (SHAEF)**,
General Dwight D. Eisenhower

Sixth Army Group,
Lieutenant General Jacob Devers

Seventh Army,
General Alexander (Sandy) Patch

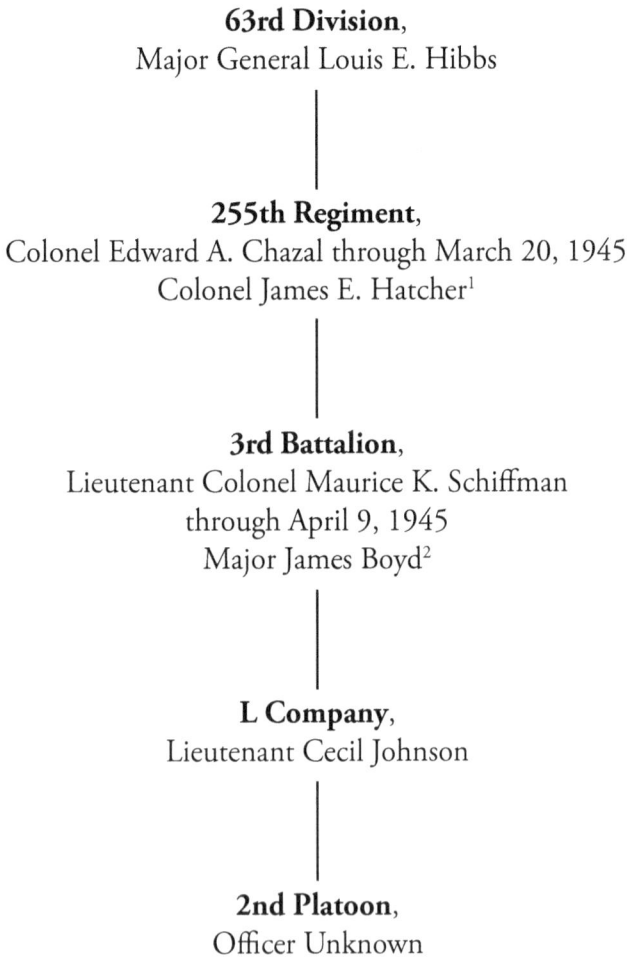

63rd Division,
Major General Louis E. Hibbs

255th Regiment,
Colonel Edward A. Chazal through March 20, 1945
Colonel James E. Hatcher[1]

3rd Battalion,
Lieutenant Colonel Maurice K. Schiffman
through April 9, 1945
Major James Boyd[2]

L Company,
Lieutenant Cecil Johnson

2nd Platoon,
Officer Unknown

APPENDIX B

Route of Joseph T. Zimmerman* [1]
February 13, 1945 – June 20, 1946

February 13, 1945 – Bliesbruck Wald (forest), Lorraine, France
February 27 – Woelfling-lés-Sarreguemines, Lorraine, France
February 27 – Sarreguemines, Lorraine, France
March 1 – Steinbach Hof (farm), France
March 1 – 1.5 miles northeast Sarreinsming at Gross Wiesing Hof (farm), France
March 12 – Sarreguemines, Lorraine, France
March 14 – Mühlenwald (forest), Saarland, Germany
March 15 – Nienhuis, Germany
March 16 – 1. 5 miles north of Neumühlhof (farm), Saarland, Germany
March 17 – Ommersheim, Saarland, Germany
March 20 – Triebscheiderhof (farm), Saarland, Germany
March 21 – Homburg, Saarland, Germany
March 23 – Limbach, Saarland, Germany
March 24 – Beeden, Saarland, Germany

* Route derived after comparison of information from multiple sources as seen in Notes.

March 25 – Höringen, Rheinland-Palatinate, Germany
March 29 – Rhine River crossing at Worms, Rheinland-Palatinate, Germany
March 29 – Lorscher Wald (forest), Hessen, Germany
March 29 – Lampertheim, Hessen, Germany
March 30 – Schriesheim, Baden-Württemberg, Germany
March 30 – Dossenheim, Baden-Württemberg, Germany
March 30 – Neckar River crossing at Neuenheim (neighborhood in Heidelberg), Baden-Württemberg, Germany
March 30 – Heidelberg, Baden-Württemberg, Germany
March 30 – Leimen, Baden-Württemberg, Germany
April 1 – Maisbach, Baden-Württemberg, Germany
April 1 – Schatthausen, Baden-Württemberg, Germany
April 2 – Zuzenhausen, Baden-Württemberg, Germany
April 2 – Hoffenheim, Baden-Württemberg, Germany
April 2 – Sinsheim, Baden-Württemberg, Germany
April 2 – Rohrbach, Sinsheim, Baden-Württemberg, Germany
April 2 – Adersbach, Sinsheim, Baden-Württemberg, Germany
April 3 – Bad Rappenau, Baden-Württemberg, Germany
April 4 – Siegelsbach, Baden-Württemberg, Germany
April 4 – Hüffenhardt, Baden-Württemberg, Germany
April 4 – Hassmersheim, Baden-Württemberg, Germany
April 4 – Neckarlez, Baden-Württemberg, Germany
April 4 – Mosbach, Baden-Württemberg, Germany
April 4 – Neckarburken, Elztal, Baden-Württemberg, Germany
April 4 – Dallau, Elztal, Baden-Württemberg, Germany
April 4 – Auerbach, Elztal, Baden-Württemberg, Germany
April 4 – Oberschefflenz, Baden-Württemberg, Germany
April 4 – Waidachshof, Baden-Württemberg, Germany
April 4 – 2 miles west of Adelsheim, Baden-Württemberg, Germany
April 5 – Möckmühl, Baden-Württemberg, Germany
April 5 – Bittelbronn, Möckmühl, Baden-Württemberg, Germany
April 6 – Neudenau, Baden-Württemberg, Germany
April 7 – Widdern, Baden-Württemberg, Germany
April 7 – Unterkessach, Baden-Württemberg, Germany

April 8 – Seehaus (farm), Baden-Württemberg, Germany
April 8 – Oberkessach, Baden-Württemberg, Germany
April 8 – Unterkessach, Baden-Württemberg, Germany
April 8 – Jagst River crossing at Widdern, Baden-Württemberg, Germany
April 8 – Harthäuser Wald (forest), Baden-Württemberg, Germany
April 9 – Lampoldshausen, Baden-Württemberg, Germany
April 9 – Buchhof (farm), Baden-Württemberg, Germany
April 10 – Crispenhofen, Baden-Württemberg, Germany
April 10 – Weissbach, Baden-Württemberg, Germany
April 11 – Niedernhall, Baden-Württemberg, Germany
April 12 – Neufels, Neuenstein, Baden-Württemberg, Germany
April 12 – Weckhof, Künzelsau, Baden-Württemberg, Germany
April 12 – Füssbach, Baden-Württemberg, Germany
April 13 – Belzhag, Baden-Württemberg, Germany
April 14 – Mangoldsall, Baden-Württemberg, Germany
April 14 – Belzhag, Baden-Württemberg, Germany
April 15 – Westernach, Baden-Württemberg, Germany
April 16 – Kupfer, Baden-Württemberg, Germany
April 17 – Kocher River crossing at Untermünkheim, Baden Württemberg, Germany
April 17 – Erlach, Baden-Württemberg, Germany
April 19 – Tüngental, Baden-Württemberg, Germany
April 20 – Lembach, Baden-Württemberg, Germany
April 21 – Rotenberg, Baden-Württemberg, Germany
April 22 – Gschwend, Baden-Württemberg, Germany
April 22 – Sulzbach-Laufen am Kocher, Baden-Württemberg, Germany
April 22 – Laufen am Kocher, Baden-Württemberg, Germany
April 22 – Seifertshofen, Baden-Württemberg, Germany
April 22 – Helpertshofen, Baden-Württemberg, Germany
April 22 – Vellbach, Baden-Württemberg, Germany
April 22 – Utzstetten, Baden-Württemberg, Germany
April 24 – Steinenkirch, Baden-Württemberg, Germany
April 24 – Ravenstein (farm), Baden-Württemberg, Germany

April 25 – Wettingen, Baden-Württemberg, Germany
April 25 – Langenau, Baden-Württemberg, Germany
April 26 – Danube River crossing at Günzburg, Baden-Württemberg, Germany
April 28 – Landsberg, Bavaria Germany
April 29 – Hurlach, Bavaria, Germany
April 29 – Oberroth, Baden-Württemberg, Germany
April 30 – Thannhausen, Baden-Württemberg, Germany
April 30 – Scheppach, Bavaria, Germany
May 1 – Gunzburg (hill), Baden-Württemberg, Germany
May 1 – Niederstotzingen, Baden-Württemberg, Germany
May 1 – Heidenheim, Baden-Württemberg, Germany
May 1 – Aalen, Baden-Württemberg, Germany
May 1 – Ellwangen, Baden-Württemberg, Germany
May 1 – Schwäbisch Hall, Baden-Württemberg, Germany
May 1 – Neuenstein, Baden-Württemberg, Germany
May 2 – Heilbronn, Baden-Württemberg, Germany
May 19 – Niederstetten, Baden-Württemberg, Germany
May 30 – Bad Mergentheim, Baden-Württemberg, Germany
October 13 – Épernay, Champagne-Ardenne, France
December 14 – Soissons, Picardie, France
January 14, 1946 – Reims, Champagne-Ardenne, France
May 31 – Paris, Île-de-France, France
June 20 – Quinter, Kansas, United States of America

BIBLIOGRAPHY

Ambrose, Stephen E. *Band of Brothers: E Company, 506th Regiment, 101st Airborne, from Normandy to Hitler's Eagle's Nest.* New York: Simon Schuster, 1990.

———. *Citizen Soldiers: The U.S. Army from the Normandy Beaches to the Bulge to the Surrender of Germany June 7, 1944, to May 7, 1945.* New York: Simon Schuster, 1997.

Anderson, C.H. "Piecemeal Employment of the 63d Infantry Division, France and Germany, December 1944 – February 1945 (Personal Experience of a Division Artillery S-3)." Regular Course, School of Combined Arms, Command and General Staff College, Fort Leavenworth, KS, 1946-1947. Accessed August 21, 2012, http://cgsc.contentdm.oclc.org/cdm/singleitem/collection/p124201coll2/id/418.

Anderson, Robert B. "My Experiences as a Combat Infantryman: 1944 – 1946." The 255th Infantry Regiment CD-ROM. The 63rd Infantry Division Association collection. Accessed June 19, 2012, http://www.63rdinfdiv.com/memorabiliapage4.html.

Ballard, Ted. *Rhineland.* Washington, D.C.: Center for Military History: GPO, CMH Publication 72-25, 1995.

Bass, Michael A., ed. "Combat: Bitche." In *The Story of the Century*, 97-131. New York: Criterion Linotyping Printing Co., Inc., 1946. Accessed August 21, 2012, http://www.marshall-foundation.org/StoryofCentury.htm.

Bedessem, Edward N. *Central Europe*. Washington, D.C.: Center for Military History: GPO, CMH Publication 72-36, 1996.

Bennett, Tony. *The Good Life: The Autobiography of Tony Bennett*. New York: Simon Schuster, 1998.

Boyd, James M., Albert G. Smith, Allan Romanoff, Chris Makas, Daniel Mendoza, Gerard J. Pepe, Israel M. Taffet, Jack Jaloski, James Keeney, Joseph Scales, Lloyd Mills, Wes Epstein. "Personnel Stories from the Men of the 255th Infantry Regiment." The 255th Infantry Regiment CD-ROM. The 63rd Infantry Division Association collection. Accessed June 19, 2012, http://www.63rdinfdiv.com/memorabiliapage4.html.

Brown, Jr., John W., Parts I and II, interview by Kevin Bing, Nicholas Molnar and Mark Segaloff, Rutgers Oral History Archives, 2004. Accessed August 21, 2012, http://oralhistory.rutgers.edu/rutgers-history/31-interviewees/833-brown-jr-john-w.

Burton, Nat. "(There'll Be Bluebirds Over) The White Cliffs of Dover." In *I'll Be Seeing You: 51 Songs of World War II*. Milwaukee, WI: Hal Leonard Corporation, 1995.

Cirillo, Roger. *Ardennes-Alsace*. Washington, D.C.: Center for Military History: GPO, CMH Publication 72-26, 1995.

Clarke, Jeffrey J., and Robert Ross Smith. *Riviera to the Rhine*. Washington, D.C.: Center for Military History: GPO, CMH Publication 7-10, 1993.

"Defense of the Saare Front." In *The Seventh United States Army Report of Operations France and Germany 1944-1945*. I and II:661-665. Edited by Aloys Graf. Nashville, TN: Battery

Press, 1988. Accessed August 21, 2012, http://www.trailblazersww2.org/history_defense_saarfront.htm.

Foster, Hugh, III. "Infantry Structure." In "The Infantry Organization for Combat, World War II." 2000. Accessed August 21, 2012, http://www.trailblazersww2.org/history_infantrystructure.htm.

Fuhrmeister, Jorg. "The Westwall in the Area of Bad Bergzabern." In *The 63rd Infantry Division Chronicles: June, 1943, to September 1945*, edited by Michael Baymor. U.S.A.: 63rd Infantry Division Association, 1991.

Garner, Joe. *We Interrupt This Broadcast: Relive the Events that Stopped Our Lives...from the Hindenburg to the Death of John F. Kennedy, Jr., Updated 2nd Ed.* Includes two audio CD-ROMs. Forward by Walter Cronkite. Nar. by Bill Kurtis. Naperville, IL: Sourcebooks, Inc., 1998.

Gove County Advocate (Quinter, KS). "Japan Surrenders to Allied Terms Tuesday Eve." August 16, 1945. Kansas Historical Society microfilm, Reel number NP1520.

Gove County Advocate (Quinter, KS). Joseph T. Zimmerman letters and notices. Kansas Historical Society microfilm, 1944 – 1946, Reel numbers NP1519 and NP1520.

Gove County Advocate (Quinter, KS). "Mrs. Adam Ziegler Rites Held at Collyer Tuesday." July 27, 1944. Kansas Historical Society microfilm, Reel number NP1519.

Hatcher, James E. *Blood and Fire: With the 63rd Infantry Division in World War II*. Radcliff, KY: 63rd Infantry Division Association, D 756.H3, 1986.

Hirsh, Michael. *The Liberators: America's Witnesses to the Holocaust*. New York: Bantam Books, 2010.

Kerins, Jack. "Combat Experiences of 1st Lt Jack Kerins 2d Platoon, D Company 255th Infantry Regiment, 63rd Infantry Division." The 255th Infantry Regiment CD-ROM. The

63rd Infantry Division Association collection. Accessed June 19, 2012, http://www.63rdinfdiv.com/memorabiliapage4. html.

Kershaw, Ian. Hitler: *1889 – 1936: Hubris*. New York: W. W. Norton Company, 1998.

"The Last German Offensive." In *The Seventh United States Army Report of Operations France and Germany 1944-1945*. I and II:559-579. Edited by Aloys Graf. Nashville, TN: Battery Press, 1988. Accessed August 21, 2012, http://www.trailblazersww2.org/history_seventh_last.htm.

Makas, Chris. "The History of B Company, 255th Infantry Regiment, 63rd Division." The 255th Infantry Regiment CD-ROM. The 63rd Infantry Division Association collection. Accessed June 19, 2012, http://www.63rdinfdiv.com/memorabiliapage4.html.

Moore, Beth. *Esther: It's Tough Being a Woman*. Nashville, TN: LifeWay Press, 2008.

Myers, Tom. Recollections of Tom Myers, 2009. Accessed August 21, 2012, http://home.scarlet.be/~tsc94696/recollection_myers.htm.

"Partial European Itinerary of 63rd Infantry Division Units and Selected Attached Units in World War II." "3rd Battalion Hq. and Hq. Co." 1944-1945. Compiled by William Scott. July 18, 1999. Accessed August 21, 2012, http://www.63rdinfdiv. com/memorabiliapage3.html.

"Plans for a Limited Offensive." In *The Seventh United States Army Report of Operations France and Germany 1944-1945*. I and II:665-669. Edited by Aloys Graf. Nashville, TN: Battery Press, 1988. Accessed August 21, 2012, http://www. trailblazersww2.org/history_limitedoffensive.htm.

United States Army. "Morning Report." 63rd Infantry Division, 255th Regiment, L Company. December 5, 1944 – May 31,

1945. The 255th Infantry Regiment Unit Morning Reports CD-ROM. The 63rd Infantry Division Association collection. Accessed June 20, 2012. http://www.63rdinfdiv.com/memorabiliapage4.html.

—————. *Regimental History: 255th Regiment, 63rd Division, January thru May, 1945* (Regimental Report of Operations). Made available by John R. Graves. The 63rd Infantry Division Association collection. Accessed June 19, 2012, http://www.63rdinfdiv.com/memorabiliapage4.html.

Zimmerman, Joseph T. Personal papers. Private collection.

Oral Histories

Sally Burgardt
Elouis Cooley (widow of JC Cooley)
Johanna Dreher
Marilyn Gabel
Winfred Hurley
Alberta Knoll
Robert McClurken
Albina Moore
Jolene Nejdl
Gordon Rintoul
Linda Simpson
Rowena Thomas
Loretta Waldman
Paul Winkler
Terrell Wright
Katherine (Kay) Younger
Darrell Zimmerman
Donald (Don) Zimmerman
Edmund (Eddie) Zimmerman

Fabian Zimmerman
Martina Zimmerman
Robert (Bob) Zimmerman
Wayne Zimmerman
William (Bill) Zimmerman

Photographs

63rd Infantry Division Association Collection
Sally Burgardt
Johanna Dreher
Naomi Rintoul
National Archives and Records Administration
Rowena Thomas
Wikimedia Commons Collection
Kay Younger
Darrell Zimmerman
Martina Zimmerman

Websites

Kaufering.com: Eleven Subcamps of Dachau Online Memorial; "Overview"; Accessed June 11, 2012.
The 100th Infantry Division website; "Lemburg"; Accessed June 11, 2012, http://www.100thww2.org/mem/lemb1.html.
Scrapbookpages.com; "Dachau Concentration Camp"; "Liberation of Dachau, 29 April 1945"; "Kaufering IV Subcamp"; Accessed June 11, 2012, http://www.scrapbookpages.com/ DachauScrapbook/DachauLiberation/KauferingIVLiberation.html.

The European Holocaust Memorial website; See esp. "Historical Facts"; "The Holocaust in the Landsberg Area"; Accessed June 11, 2012, buergervereinigung-landsberg.org.

The United States Holocaust Memorial Museum website; "Holocaust Encyclopedia"; "The 63rd Infantry Division"; Accessed June 11, 2012, http://www.ushmm.org.

U.S. Army Center of Military History website; "63d Infantry Division" entry; Accessed June 11, 2012, http://www.history. army.mil/documents/ETO-OB/63ID-ETO.htm.

World War II Troop Ships website; "1945 Troop Ship Crossings: January to June"; Accessed June 11, 2012, ww2troopships. com.

NOTES

Chapter One

1. Beth Moore, *Esther: It's Tough Being a Woman* (Nashville, TN: LifeWay Press, 2008), 171.
2. United States Army, Regimental History: *255th Regiment, 63rd Division, January thru May, 1945* (Regimental Report of Operations), Made available by John R. Graves (The 63rd Infantry Division Association collection): Report for February 13, 1945, http://www.63rdinfdiv.com/memorabiliapage4.html.
3. United States Army, "Morning Report," 63rd Infantry Division, 255th Regiment, L Company, December 5, 1944 – May 31, 1945, The 255th Infantry Regiment Unit Morning Reports CD-ROM (The 63rd Infantry Division Association collection), Report for February 13, 1945, http://www.63rdinfdiv.com/memorabiliapage4.html.
4. U. S. Army, *255th Regimental History*, Report for February 13, 1945 – February 15, 1945.
5. U.S. Army, "Morning Report," Report for February 13, 1945.
6. U. S. Army, *255th Regimental History*, Report for February, 13, 1945 – February 15, 1945.
7. Ibid., Report for February 15, 1945.
8. Robert B. Anderson, "My Experiences as a Combat Infantryman: 1944 – 1946," The 255th Infantry Regiment CD-ROM (The 63rd Infantry Division Association collection): 12, http://www.63rdinfdiv.com/memorabiliapage4.html.
9. U. S. Army, *255th Regimental History*, Report for February 14, 1945 – February 15, 1945.

10. U. S. Army, *255th Regimental History*, Report for February 15, 1945. Sentence portion "Company K met…"; James M. Boyd, et al. "Personnel Stories from the Men of the 255th Infantry Regiment," The 255th Infantry Regiment CD-ROM (The 63rd Infantry Division Association collection): 1, http://www.63rdinfdiv.com/memorabiliapage4.html. Sentence portion "I Company experienced…"

11. U. S. Army, *255th Regimental History*, Report for February 15, 1945.

12. Ibid., Report for February 15, 1945.

13. U.S. Army, "Morning Report," Report for February 16 – 17, 1945 and March 4, 1945.

14. Anderson, "My Experiences," 12.

15. U. S. Army, *255th Regimental History*, Report for February 15, 1945 (evening).

16. Robert Anderson, "My Experiences," 12.

17. U. S. Army, *255th Regimental History*, Report for February 16, 1945.

18. Jeffrey J. Clark and Robert Ross Smith, *Riviera to the Rhine* (Washington, D.C.: Center for Military History: GPO, CMH Publication 7-10, 1993), 565-566.

19. U. S. Army, *255th Regimental History*, Report for February 16, 1945.

20. Chris Makas, "The History of B Company, 255th Infantry Regiment, 63rd Division," The 255th Infantry Regiment CD-ROM (The 63rd Infantry Division Association collection): 6, http://www.63rdinfdiv.com/memorabiliapage4.html.

21. U. S. Army, *255th Regimental History*, Report for February 16, 1945.

22. Robert Anderson, "My Experiences," 12.

23. Ibid., 12-13.

24. Makas, "History of B Company," 6.

25. Robert Anderson, "My Experiences," 12-13.

26. Joe Garner, *We Interrupt This Broadcast: Relive the Events that Stopped Our Lives…from the Hindenburg to the Death of John F. Kennedy, Jr., Updated Second Ed.*, Includes two audio CD-ROMS, Forward by Walter Cronkite, Nar. By Bill Kurtis, (Naperville, IL: Sourcebooks, Inc., 1998), Disc 1, track 3.

27. Stephen E. Ambrose, *Citizen Soldiers: The U.S. Army from the Normandy Beaches to the Bulge to the Surrender of Germany June 7, 1944, to May 7, 1945* (New York: Simon & Schuster, 1997), 50-51.

28. Ambrose, *Citizen Soldiers*, 86.

29. Ibid., 71.

30. Ibid., 96.

31. Rowena Thomas (sister of Joseph T. Zimmerman), interview by the author, 2011; Sally Burgardt (sister of Joseph T. Zimmerman), interview by the author, 2011.

32. Alberta Knoll (sister of Joseph T. Zimmerman), interview by the author, 2011.

33. Johanna Dreher (sister of Joseph T. Zimmerman), interview by the author, 2010.

34. Fabian Zimmerman (brother of Joseph T. Zimmerman), interview by the author, 2011.

35. "Mrs. Adam Ziegler Rites Held at Collyer Tuesday," *Gove County Advocate* (Quinter, KS), July 27, 1944, (Kansas Historical Society microfilm), Reel number NP1519.
36. President Harry Truman to Joseph T. Zimmerman, letter of commendation (form letter), private collection.
37. Knoll, interview.
38. Tom Myers, Recollections of Tom Myers (2009), http://home.scarlet.be/~tsc94696/recollection_myers.htm.
39. James E. Hatcher, Blood and Fire: With the 63rd Infantry Division in World War II (Radcliff, KY: 63rd Infantry Division Association, D 756.H3, 1986), 3.
40. Ambrose, Citizen Soldiers, 105-106.
41. Ibid., 116.

Chapter Two

1. Ambrose, *Citizen Soldiers*, 38-39.
2. Ibid., 165.
3. Ibid., 184-185.
4. Ibid., 197.
5. Ibid., 393.
6. *Gove County Advocate* (Quinter, KS), January 4, 1945, notice on Joseph T. Zimmerman, (Kansas Historical Society, microfilm), Reel number NP1519.
7. Myers, Recollections.
8. Myers, Recollections.
9. Ibid.
10. Myers, Recollections. Sentence portion "black…night"; World War II Troop Ships website, "1945 Troop Ship Crossings: January to June," Accessed June 11, 2012, ww2troopships.com. Sentence portion *"Queen Mary."*

Chapter Three

1. Hatcher, *63rd Infantry Division*, 7.
2. Troop Ships website, "Troop Ship Crossings."
3. Robert Anderson, "My Experiences," 4.
4. John W. Brown, Jr., Parts I and II, interview by Kevin Bing, Nicholas Molnar and Mark Segaloff (Rutgers Oral History Archives, 2004): Pt. 1, http://oralhistory.rutgers.edu/rutgers-history/31-interviewees/833-brown-jr-john-w.
5. *Gove County Advocate* (Quinter, KS), vol. 43, June 27, 1946, notice on Joseph T. Zimmerman, (Kansas Historical Society, microfilm), Reel number NP1520.
6. Troop Ships website, "Troop Ship Crossings," Ship information for January 24, 1945.
7. Myers, Recollections.
8. Fabian Zimmerman, interview.

9. Burgardt, interview.
10. Fabian Zimmerman, interview. Current and two preceding paragraphs.
11. Ambrose, *Citizen Soldiers*, 276-277. Entire paragraph.
12. Boyd et al., "Personal Stories," 14. Particular information comes from the memoirs of Jack Jaloski.
13. Dreher, interview.
14. Albina Moore (sister of Joseph T. Zimmerman), interview by the author, 2011.
15. Dreher, interview.
16. Fabian Zimmerman, interview.
17. U.S. Army, "Morning Report," Report for February 13, 1945. Sentence portion "He and eighteen other men"; U. S. Army, *255th Regimental History*, Report for February 9-10, 1945, February 13, 1945. Sentence portion "in the Bliesbrucken Woods."
18. Brown, interview, Pt. 1.
19. Ambrose, *Citizen Soldiers*, 277-278.
20. Roger Cirillo, *Ardennes-Alsace* (Washington, D.C.: Center for Military History: GPO, CMH Publication 72-26, 1995), 39-40.
21. Ted Ballard, *Rhineland* (Washington, D.C.: Center for Military History: GPO, CMH Publication 72-25, 1995), 6.
22. Michael A. Bass, ed., "Combat: Bitche," In *The Story of the Century*, 98 (New York: Criterion Linotyping Printing Co., Inc., 1946), http://www.marshallfoundation.org/StoryofCentury.htm.
23. "The Last German Offensive," In *The Seventh United States Army Report of Operations France and Germany 1944-1945*, I and II:559-579, Edited by Aloys Graf (Nashville, TN: Battery Press, 1988), http://www.trailblazersww2.org/history_seventh_last.htm.
24. Cirillo, *Ardennes-Alsace*, 42.
25. U. S. Army Center of Military History website, "63d Infantry Division" entry, Accessed June 11, 2012, http://www.history.army.mil/documents/ETO-OB/63ID-ETO.htm.
26. The 100th Infantry Division website, "Lemburg," Accessed June 11, 2012, http://www.100thww2.org/mem/lemb1.html.
27. Cirillo, *Ardennes-Alsace*, 52.

Chapter Four

1. Ambrose, *Citizen Soldiers*, 272.
2. Stephen E. Ambrose, *Band of Brothers: E Company, 506th Regiment, 101st Airborne, from Normandy to Hitler's Eagle's Nest* (New York: Simon Schuster, 1990),316.

3. "Defense of the Saare Front," *In The Seventh United States Army Report of Operations France and Germany 1944-1945*, I and II:661-665. Edited by Aloys Graf (Nashville, TN: Battery Press, 1988), http://www.trailblazersww2.org/history_defense_saarfront.htm.

4. Ambrose, *Citizen Soldiers*, 258. Sentence portion "As the most bitter…dipped below zero"

5. Jack Kerins, "Combat Experiences of 1st Lt Jack Kerins 2d Platoon, D Company 255th Infantry Regiment, 63rd Infantry Division," The 255th Infantry Regiment CD-ROM (The 63rd Infantry Division Association collection): 7, http://www.63rdinfdiv.com/memorabiliapage4.html.

6. C. H. Anderson, "Piecemeal Employment of the 63d Infantry Division, France and Germany, December 1944 – February 1945 (Personal Experience of a Division Artillery S-3)," Regular Course, School of Combined Arms, Command and General Staff College (Fort Leavenworth, KS, 1946-1947):12, http://cgsc.contentdm.oclc.org/cdm/singleitem/collection/p124201coll2/id/418.

7. Kerins, "Combat Experiences," 18.

8. Robert Anderson, "My Experiences," 9.

9. Ambrose, *Citizen Soldiers*, 265-266.

10. Robert Anderson, "My Experiences," 11. Sentence portion "As the days warmed and the melting snow trickled into the hole"

11. U.S. Army, "Morning Report," Reports for February, 1945, and beginning of March, 1945.

12. Ambrose, *Citizen Soldiers*, 264.

13. Ibid.

14. Bass, "Combat: Bitche," 121-122.

15. Fabian Zimmerman, interview.

16. Ambrose, *Citizen Soldiers*, 414.

17. Boyd et al., "Personal Stories," 12. Particular information comes from the memoirs of Gerard J. Pepe.

18. U.S. Army, "Morning Report," Report for February 27, 1945.

19. Kerins, "Combat Experiences," 18.

20. Ibid., 9.

21. Hatcher, *63rd Infantry Division*, 47.

22. U.S. Army, "Morning Report," Report for March 1, 1945. Sentence portion "Through the morning…Wiesinger Hof, France."; U. S. Army, *255th Regimental History*, Report for March 1 – March 2, 1945. Sentence portion "to relieve…high ground."

23. Joseph T. Zimmerman, "I Love You," poem, March 1, 1945, private collection.

24. U. S. Army, *255th Regimental History*, Report for March 3 (night) – March 4, 1945.

25. U.S. Army, "Morning Report," Report for March 12, 1945.

26. Robert Anderson, "My Experiences," 13.

27. Kerins, "Combat Experiences," 9.

Chapter Five

1. Kerins, "Combat Experiences," 7.
2. Ambrose, *Citizen Soldiers*, 161-162.
3. Ian Kershaw, *Hitler: 1889 – 1936: Hubris* (New York: W. W. Norton Company, 1998), 302-311.
4. Kershaw, *Hitler*, 333-334.
5. Jorg Fuhrmeister, "The Westwall in the Area of Bad Bergzabern," In *The 63rd Infantry Division Chronicles: June, 1943, to September 1945*, edited by Michael Baymor (U.S.A.: 63rd Infantry Division Association, 1991), 3.
6. Boyd et al., "Personal Stories," 19. Particular information comes from the memoirs of Lloyd Mills.
7. U.S. Army, "Morning Report," Report for March 14, 1945. Sentence portion "Finally, at 8:15 p.m…two hours later"; U. S. Army, *255th Regimental History*, Report for March 7-8, March 15, 1945. Sentence portion "arrived…in the Muhlenwald (forest)."
8. Robert Anderson, "My Experiences," 16.
9. Kerins, "Combat Experiences," 9.
10. Ibid., 10.
11. Hatcher, *63rd Infantry Division*, 57.
12. Kerins, "Combat Experiences," 10.
13. Makas, "History of B Company," 9.
14. Hatcher, *63rd Infantry Division*, 61. Sentence portion "difficult terrain."
15. Robert Anderson, "My Experiences," 15. Sentence portion "explosions of… shells."
16. Paul Winkler (veteran of Company L), interview by author, 2010.
17. U. S. Army, *255th Regimental History*, Report for March 15, 1945.
18. Ibid.
19. Robert Anderson, "My Experiences," 15.
20. U.S. Army, "Morning Report," Report for March 16, 1945. Sentence portion "That day"; Winkler, interview. Sentence portion "Winkler went…before being shot."
21. U. S. Army, *255th Regimental History*, Report for March 15, 1945.
22. Robert Anderson, "My Experiences," 15.
23. U. S. Army, *255th Regimental History*, Report for March 16, 1945.
24. U. S. Army, "Morning Report," Reports for March 16 – March 19, 1945, and March 28, 1945.
25. U. S. Army, *255th Regimental History*, Report for March 17, 1945.
26. Robert Anderson, "My Experiences," 15
27. Hatcher, *63rd Infantry Division*, 71.
28. U. S. Army, *255th Regimental History*, Report for March 18 – March 19, 1945.
29. Hatcher, *63rd Infantry Division*, 72.
30. Brown, interview, Pt. 2.

31. U. S. Army, *255th Regimental History*, Report for March 18 – March 19, 1945.

32. Hatcher, *63rd Infantry Division*, 73.

Chapter Six

1. Clark and Smith, *Riviera to the Rhine*, 566-567.

2. Ambrose, *Citizen Soldiers*, 452-454.

3. Robert Anderson, "My Experiences," 16.

4. Brown, interview, Pt. 1.

5. U.S. Army, "Morning Report," Report for March 21, 1945.

6. Hatcher, *63rd Infantry Division*, 76.

7. Robert Anderson, "My Experiences," 18.

8. Kerins, "Combat Experiences," 12.

9. Hatcher, *63rd Infantry Division*, 77.

10. Robert Anderson, "My Experiences," 16.

11. U.S. Army, "Morning Report," Reports for March 24, 1945, and March 26, 1945.

12. Fabian Zimmerman, interview.

13. Kay Younger (sister of Joseph T. Zimmerman), interview by the author, 2011.

14. Robert McClurken (veteran of Company L), interview by the author, 2010.

15. Hatcher, *63rd Infantry Division*, 79.

16. Ibid., 77-79. Information from quote and entire paragraph.

17. U.S. Army, "Morning Report," Report for 31, 1945.

18. Hatcher, *63rd Infantry Division*, 79.

19. Kerins, "Combat Experiences," 12.

20. Hatcher, *63rd Infantry Division*, 82.

21. Ambrose, *Band of Brothers*, 260.

22. Hatcher, *63rd Infantry Division*, 81-82)

23. U. S. Army, *255th Regimental History*, Report for March 28, 1945 and March 30, 1945.

24. Hatcher, *63rd Infantry Division*, 81.

25. U. S. Army, *255th Regimental History*, Report for March 29, 1945 and March 30, 1945.

26. Brown, interview, Pt. 2.

27. Ibid.

28. U. S. Army, *255th Regimental History*, Report for March 28, 1945 and March 30, 1945.

29. Hatcher, *63rd Infantry Division*, 84-85.

30. Robert Anderson, "My Experiences," 17.

31. Kerins, "Combat Experiences," 12.

Chapter Seven

1. Hatcher, *63rd Infantry Division*, 4.
2. U. S. Army, *255th Regimental History*, Operation Instructions number 23 and Field Order number 4 on April 1, 1945.
3. Robert Anderson, "My Experiences," 17.
4. Don Zimmerman (son of Joseph T. Zimmerman), interview by the author, Interview number 5, 2011.
5. U. S. Army, *255th Regimental History*, Report for April 1, 1945, 1245 – end of day.
6. Ibid., Report for April 1, 1945, 1500 – 2000.
7. Hatcher, *63rd Infantry Division*, 87.
8. U. S. Army, *255th Regimental History*, Report for April 1, 1945, 1500 – 2000.
9. Robert Anderson, "My Experiences," 17.
10. U. S. Army, *255th Regimental History*, Report for April 1, 1945, 1500 – end of day.
11. Dreher, interview.
12. Terrell Wright (veteran of Company L), interview by the author, 2010.
13. Knoll, interview.
14. Dreher, interview.
15. Eddie Zimmerman (brother of Joseph T. Zimmerman), interview by the author, 2011.
16. Hatcher, *63rd Infantry Division*, 91.
17. Fabian Zimmerman, interview.
18. Robert Anderson, "My Experiences," 17. Sentence portion "blankets…K-rations"
19. U. S. Army, *255th Regimental History*, Operations Report number 29 on April 2, 1945 and report for April 2, 1945, 0600 – 0835.
20. Ibid., Report for April 2, 1945. Sentence portion "The men worked…to clear the village"
21. Ibid., Report for April 3, 1945.
22. Hatcher, *63rd Infantry Division*, 92.
23. Ibid., 93.
24. U. S. Army, *255th Regimental History*, Report for April 3, 1945.
25. Robert Anderson, "My Experiences," 18.
26. U. S. Army, *255th Regimental History*, Report for April 3, 1945.
27. Robert Anderson, "My Experiences," 18.
28. Ibid., 19. Sentence portion "Wearing their field jackets…early spring"; U. S. Army, *255th Regimental History*, Report for April 4, 1945. Sentence portion "Love Company…with I and K Companies."
29. U. S. Army, *255th Regimental History*, Report for April 5, 1945.
30. Robert Anderson, "My Experiences," 19.
31. U. S. Army, *255th Regimental History*, Report for April 6, 1945.

32. Robert Anderson, "My Experiences," 19. Sentence portion "The day had been rainy since breakfast"
33. Robert Anderson, "My Experiences," 19-20. Sentence portion "Double guards were posted that night"; U. S. Army, *255th Regimental History*, Report for April 6, 1945. Sentence portion "heavy mortar fire...sporadic pop of sniper rifles... through the darkness."
34. U. S. Army, *255th Regimental History*, Report for April 6, 1945.
35. Robert Anderson, "My Experiences," 21.
36. Hatcher, *63rd Infantry Division*, 95.
37. Dreher, interview.
38. U. S. Army, *255th Regimental History*, Report for April 6, 1945.
39. Hatcher, *63rd Infantry Division*, 95.
40. U.S. Army, "Morning Report," Report for April 7, 1945.
41. Ibid., Report for April 7, 1945.
42. U. S. Army, *255th Regimental History*, Report for April 8, 1945.
43. Ibid.
44. Robert Anderson, "My Experiences," 20.
45. U. S. Army, *255th Regimental History*, Report for April 8, 1945.
46. Hatcher, 63rd Infantry Division, 98.
47. U. S. Army, *255th Regimental History*, Report for April 8, 1945.
48. Ibid.

Chapter Eight

1. Hugh Foster, III, "Infantry Structure," In "The Infantry Organization for Combat, World War II" (2000), http://www.trailblazersww2.org/history_infantrystructure.htm.
2. Hatcher, *63rd Infantry Division*, 105-106.
3. U. S. Army, *255th Regimental History*, Report for April 9, 1945.
4. U.S. Army, "Morning Report," Reports for April 9, 1945, and April 15, 1945.
5. Robert Anderson, "My Experiences," 21. Sentence portion "soldiers sat...over the hot meal"
6. Hatcher, *63rd Infantry Division*, 100.
7. U. S. Army, *255th Regimental History*, Report for April 11, 1945.
8. Hatcher, *63rd Infantry Division*, 101-102.
9. Robert Anderson, "My Experiences," 22.
10. U. S. Army, *255th Regimental History*, Report for April 11, 1945.
11. Robert Anderson, "My Experiences," 22.
12. U. S. Army, *255th Regimental History*, Report for April 12, 1945.
13. Robert Anderson, "My Experiences," 22.
14. U. S. Army, *255th Regimental History*, Report for April 13, 1945.
15. Ibid., Reports for April, 1945.
16. Robert Anderson, "My Experiences," 24.

17. U. S. Army, *255th Regimental History*, Report for April 15, 1945.
18. Brown, interview, Pt. 2.
19. U. S. Army, *255th Regimental History*, Report for April 14, 1945.
20. Joseph T. Zimmerman to Zimmerman family, letter, Germany, April 14, 1945, in *Gove County Advocate* (Quinter, KS), May 3, 1945, (Kansas Historical Society, microfilm), reel NP1520.
21. Knoll, interview.
22. Loretta Waldman (sister of Joseph T. Zimmerman), interview by the author, 2011.
23. Michael Hirsh, *The Liberators: America's Witnesses to the Holocaust* (New York: Bantam Books, 2010), 19-22.
24. Burgardt, interview.
25. Hatcher, *63rd Infantry Division*, 115. Sentence portion "By midnight…high ground"; U.S. Army, "Morning Report," Report for April 16, 1945. Sentence portion "at Mangoldsall"; Robert Anderson, "My Experiences," 22. Sentence portion "set up a defensive perimeter…that night."
26. Robert Anderson, "My Experiences," 23.
27. Hatcher, *63rd Infantry Division*, 115-116.
28. U. S. Army, *255th Regimental History*, Report for April 15, 1945.
29. Hatcher, *63rd Infantry Division*, 115.
30. U. S. Army, *255th Regimental History*, Report for April 15, 1945.
31. Hatcher, *63rd Infantry Division*, 116.
32. Ibid.
33. Ibid., 116-118.
34. Robert Anderson, "My Experiences," 24.
35. Hatcher, *63rd Infantry Division*, 114.
36. Ibid., 122.
37. Ibid., 123.
38. Robert Anderson, "My Experiences," 26.
39. U. S. Army, *255th Regimental History*, Report for April 26, 1945.
40. Hatcher, *63rd Infantry Division*, 127-128.
41. Ibid., 129.
42. Kerins, "Combat Experiences," 3.

Chapter Nine

1. Kerins, "Combat Experiences," 9.
2. Ibid., 15.
3. Hirsh, *The Liberators*, 168.
4. Kerins, "Combat Experiences," 15.
5. U. S. Army, *255th Regimental History*, Report for April 28, 1945.
6. Hirsh, *The Liberators*, 167.

7. Boyd et al., "Personal Stories," 20. Particular information comes from the memoirs of Wes Epstein.
8. U. S. Army, *255th Regimental History*, Report for April 28, 1945.
9. Hirsh, *The Liberators*, 169.
10. Edward N. Bedessem, *Central Europe* (Washington, D.C.: Center for Military History: GPO, CMH Publication 72-36, 1996), 26.
11. Brown, interview, Pt. 2.
12. Ambrose, *Citizen Soldiers*, 464.
13. Hirsh, *The Liberators*, 168.
14. The United States Holocaust Memorial Museum website, "Holocaust Encyclopedia," "The 63rd Infantry Division," Accessed June 11, 2012, ushmm.org.
15. Kerins, "Combat Experiences," 15.
16. Boyd et al., "Personal Stories," 20. Particular information comes from the memoirs of Wes Epstein.
17. Hatcher, *63rd Infantry Division*, 131.
18. Scrapbookpages.com, "Dachau Concentration Camp," "Liberation of Dachau, 29 April 1945," "Kaufering IV Subcamp," Accessed June 11, 2012, http://www.scrapbookpages.com/DachauScrapbook/DachauLiberation/KauferingIVLiberation.html.
19. Kaufering.com: Eleven Subcamps of Dachau Online Memorial, "Overview," Accessed June 11, 2012.
20. The European Holocaust Memorial website, See esp. "Historical Facts," "The Holocaust in the Landsberg Area," Accessed June 11, 2012, buergervereinigunglandsberg.org.
21. Holocaust Museum website, "63rd Division."
22. Hirsh, *The Liberators*, 162.
23. Ambrose, *Citizen Soldiers*, 464.
24. Hatcher, *63rd Infantry Division*, 132-133.
25. Kerins, "Combat Experiences," 16.
26. McClurken, interview.
27. Winkler, interview.
28. Wright, interview.
29. Gordon Rintoul (veteran of Company L), interview by the author, 2009.
30. Ibid.
31. Ibid.
32. Ambrose, *Citizen Soldiers*, 464.
33. U. S. Army, *255th Regimental History*, Report for April 28, 1945.
34. Robert Anderson, "My Experiences," 27.
35. Ambrose, *Citizen Soldiers*, 280-281.

Chapter Ten

1. Hatcher, *63rd Infantry Division*, 133.
2. Clark and Smith, *Riviera to the Rhine*, 565.
3. U.S. Army, "Morning Report," Report for May 2, 1945.
4. Robert Anderson, "My Experiences," 27. Sentence portion "the men took turns…and standing"; U. S. Army, *255th Regimental History*, Report for April 29, 1945. Sentence portion "twenty miles per hour."
5. U.S. Army, "Morning Report," Report for May 2, 1945. Sentence portion "thirteen hour journey"
6. Robert Anderson, "My Experiences," 27-28.
7. Fabian Zimmerman, interview.
8. U. S. Army, *255th Regimental History*, Report for April 30, 1945.
9. Boyd et al., "Personal Stories," 15. Particular information comes from the memoirs of James Boyd.
10. Hatcher, *63rd Infantry Division*, 134.
11. Rintoul, interview.
12. Boyd et al., "Personal Stories," 19. Particular information comes from the memoirs of Lloyd Mills.
13. Robert Anderson, "My Experiences," 28.
14. U.S. Army, "Morning Report," Reports for May, 1945.
15. Makas, "History of B Company," 13.
16. Joseph T. Zimmerman to Zimmerman family, letter, Bad Mergentheim, Germany, May 30, 1945, in *Gove County Advocate* (Quinter, KS), June 21, 1945, (Kansas Historical Society, microfilm), reel NP1520.
17. "Japan Surrenders to Allied Terms Tuesday Eve," *Gove County Advocate* (Quinter, KS), August 16, 1945, (Kansas Historical Society microfilm), Reel number NP1520.
18. Joseph T. Zimmerman to Martina Ziegler, Epernay, October 13, 1945, private collection.
19. Waldman, interview.
20. Joseph T. Zimmerman to Zimmerman family, letter, France, December 14, 1945, in *Gove County Advocate* (Quinter, KS), vol. 43, January 10, 1946, (Kansas Historical Society, microfilm), reel NP1520.
21. Burgardt, interview.
22. Moore, interview.
23. Joseph T. Zimmerman to Zimmerman family, letter, Reims, France, January 14, 1946, in *Gove County Advocate* (Quinter, KS), February 7, 1946, (Kansas Historical Society, microfilm), Reel number NP1520.
24. *Gove County Advocate* (Quinter, KS), February 21, 1946, notice on Joseph T. Zimmerman, (Kansas Historical Society, microfilm), Reel number NP1520.

25. Joseph T. Zimmerman, "A Peaceful Day," poem within letter to family, Reims, France, January 14, 1946, in *Gove County Advocate* (Quinter, KS), February 7, 1946, (Kansas Historical Society, microfilm), Reel number NP1520.

Chapter Eleven

1. Truman to Zimmerman, private collection.
2. Boyd et al., "Personal Stories," 19. Particular information comes from the memoirs of Lloyd Mills.
3. Waldman, interview.
4. *Gove County Advocate* (Quinter, KS), vol. 43, June 6, 1946, notice on Joseph T. Zimmerman, (Kansas Historical Society, microfilm), Reel number NP1520.
5. Robert Anderson, "My Experiences," 29.
6. Nat Burton, "(There'll Be Bluebirds Over) The White Cliffs of Dover," In I'll Be Seeing You: 51 Songs of World War II. Milwaukee, WI: Hal Leonard Corporation, 1995. (41)
7. Dreher, interview.
8. *Gove County Advocate* (Quinter, KS), vol. 43, June 6, 1946, notice on Joseph T. Zimmerman, (Kansas Historical Society, microfilm), Reel number NP1520.
9. Knoll, interview.
10. Thomas, interview.
11. Moore, interview. Sentence portion "The fun-loving boy…serious man"; Burgardt, interview. Sentence portion "sometimes broke down crying"; Eddie Zimmerman, interview. Sentence portion "jumped at loud sounds."
12. Fabian Zimmerman, interview.
13. Thomas, interview.
14. Joseph T. Zimmerman, "Civilian Life," private collection.

Chapter Twelve

1. Linda Simpson (niece of Joseph T. Zimmerman), interview by the author, 2011.
2. Ibid.
3. Dreher, interview.
4. *Gove County Advocate* (Quinter, KS), vol. 43, November 24, 1946, notice on Ziegler-Zimmerman wedding, (Kansas Historical Society, microfilm), Reel number NP1520.
5. Fabian Zimmerman, interview.
6. Waldman, interview.
7. Joseph T. Zimmerman, "My Darling," private collection.
8. Don Zimmerman, interview.
9. "State Board for Vocational Education," application for farm training, private collection.

10. Bob Zimmerman (son of Joseph T. Zimmerman), interview by the author, 2011.
11. Don Zimmerman, interview.

Chapter Thirteen

1. Dreher, interview.
2. Thomas, interview.
3. Simpson, interview
4. Darrell Zimmerman (son of Joseph T. Zimmerman), interview by the author, 2011.
5. Bill Zimmerman (son of Joseph T. Zimmerman), interview by the author, 2011.
6. Darrell Zimmerman, interview.
7. Don Zimmerman, interview.
8. Ibid.
9. Darrell Zimmerman, interview.

10. Jolene Nejdl (daughter of Joseph T. Zimmerman), interview by the author, 2011.
11. Darrell Zimmerman, interview. Sentence portion "'Well, hello, Snowball'"; Robert Zimmerman, interview. Sentence portion "as he limped…puffing on a cigar."
12. Don Zimmerman, interview.
13. Darrell Zimmerman, interview.
14. Nejdl, interview; Marilyn Gabel (daughter of Joseph T. Zimmerman), interview by the author, 2011.
15. Gabel, interview.
16. Simpson, interview.
17. Darrell Zimmerman, interview.
18. Bill Zimmerman, interview.
19. Don Zimmerman, interview.
20. Simpson, interview.
21. Wayne Zimmerman (son of Joseph T. Zimmerman), interview by the author, 2011.
22. Fabian Zimmerman, interview.
23. Darrell Zimmerman, interview. Preceding three paragraphs.
24. Don Zimmerman, interview.
25. Ibid.
26. Ibid.
27. Nejdl, interview.
28. Bill Zimmerman, interview.
29. Don Zimmerman, interview.
30. Gabel, interview

31. Don Zimmerman, interview.
32. Bob Zimmerman, interview.
33. Don Zimmerman, interview.
34. Ibid.
35. Joseph T. Zimmerman, untitled poem, private collection.
36. Nejdl, interview.
37. Moore interview. Sentence portion "real thoughtful...hurting us"; Waldman interview. Sentence portion "good manners...lose temper."
38. Waldman, interview.
39. Knoll, interview.
40. Moore, interview.
41. Moore, interview.

Chapter Fourteen

1. Thomas, interview.
2. Dreher, interview.
3. Martina Zimmerman to railroad employers of Joseph T. Zimmerman, letter, private collection.
4. Moore, interview.
5. Younger, interview.
6. Thomas, interview.
7. Ibid.
8. Ibid., Paragraph portion "drive into a ditch...tumor had been growing for a long time."
9. Fabian Zimmerman, interview.
10. Thomas, interview.
11. Waldman, interview.
12. Don Zimmerman, interview.
13. Ibid.
14. Darrell Zimmerman, interview.
15. Nejdl, interview.
16. Bob Zimmerman, interview.
17. Thomas, interview.
18. Bill Zimmerman, interview. Sentence portion "Bill enjoyed learning...work interesting"
19. Ibid.
20. Don Zimmerman, interview.
21. Thomas, interview. Existing and preceding two paragraphs.
22. Joseph T. Zimmerman, "Friendship," private collection.
23. Fabian Zimmerman, interview.

24. Fabian Zimmerman, interview.
25. Dreher, interview.
26. Fabian Zimmerman, interview.

Chapter Fifteen

1. Knoll, interview.
2. Bob Zimmerman, interview.
3. Darrell Zimmerman, interview. Existing and preceding paragraph.
4. Bob Zimmerman, interview.
5. Bill Zimmerman, interview.
6. Burgardt, interview.
7. Don Zimmerman, interview.
8. Burgardt, interview.
9. Younger, interview.
10. Burgardt, interview.
11. Fabian Zimmerman, interview.
12. Simpson, interview.
13. Gabel, interview.
14. Fabian Zimmerman, interview.
15. Bob Zimmerman, interview.
16. Don Zimmerman, interview.

Epilogue

1. Bob Zimmerman, interview.
2. Dreher, interview.
3. Thomas, interview.
4. Bill Zimmerman, interview.

Appendix A

1. U. S. Army, *255th Regimental History*, Report for March 20, 1945.
2. Hatcher, *63rd Infantry Division*, 98.

Appendix B

1. *Gove County Advocate* (Quinter, KS), Joseph T. Zimmerman letters and notices, Reel numbers NP1519 and NP1520; Hatcher, *63rd Infantry Division*; Joseph T. Zimmerman, correspondence, private collection; "Partial European Itinerary of 63rd Infantry Division Units and Selected Attached Units in World War II," "3rd Battalion Hq. and Hq. Co.," 1944-1945, Compiled by William Scott,

216

July 18, 1999, http://www.63rdinfdiv.com/memorabiliapage3.html; U.S. Army, "Morning Report," Reports for February, 1945 – May, 1945; U. S. Army, *255th Regimental History*;